This is Southern Region Central Division

Contents

1 Introduction
3 The London, Brighton & South Coast Railway
10 The Atmospheric Experiments and Early Electrification
14 Central Division Steam *photo feature*
17 Main Line Electrification and the Pullmans
20 Modern Rolling Stock
26 Specials on the Central Division *photo feature*
30 Brighton Line Modernisation
39 Brighton Line Resignalling
44 Branches No More *photo feature*
46 The East Sussex Branches and the Oxted Line
50 The Bluebell Railway
54 Central Division Headcodes

Front cover: Class 423 unit No 7873 forms the 15.23 Victoria to Bognor service on 23 April 1981. *Les Bertram*

Below right: This scene epitomises today's Central Division, as Class 421 No 7399 leads a 12-coach Victoria-Littlehampton service south of Balcombe on the morning of 6 May 1980. Relatively modern rolling stock, ostensibly 'Inter-City' although lacking facilities such as air conditioning now standard elsewhere in the country, heads through attractive leafy countryside on a line relied upon by the bulk of its passengers to link rural domesticity with urban employment. *Brian Morrison*

First published 1982

ISBN 0 7110 1188 5

Published by

IAN ALLAN LTD

Terminal House Shepperton TW17 8AS England

Telephone: Walton-on-Thames 28950

Printed by Ian Allan Printing Ltd at their works at Coombelands in Runnymede, England

The Central Division has been described as a herring bone, not only by disgruntled commuters sweating in stuffy summer evening trains or freezing on bleak winter mornings awaiting trains delayed by ice or fog who liken the system to 'stinking fish', but also by Bob Mackmurdie, Divisional Manager, Central Division, Southern Region, when referring to the physical appearance of the system over which he is in control.

The line from London to Brighton is the backbone of the Central Division, which covers an area of England to the south of London bounded on the west by Havant (Hants) and Dorking (Surrey), to the east by Uckfield and Hastings (Sussex) and, to the south by the sea. It forms a major part of the most intensively used suburban service in the world, and carries over 200,000 commuters to and from the capital each weekday, as well as substantial passenger traffic to seaside resorts and a growing percentage of the itself increasing number of air passengers travelling to and from Gatwick Airport.

Such passengers on the Central Division travel, in the main, on an electrified railway system that has changed little since third-rail electrification was extended to the coast by the Southern Railway between 1932 and 1939. The prewar rolling stock was replaced in the 1960s and early 1970s by new main line and semi-fast trains, but otherwise few major changes took place on the Division until London Bridge was rebuilt and resignalled in the mid-1970s. This major rebuilding caused some inconvenience to the travelling public, but such inconvenience was minimised by the major works being carried out at weekends when traffic was light and could be diverted to Victoria. The second stage of the Brighton line modernisation — involving the rebuilding of Victoria and the resignalling of the main line throughout — has just begun, and is of such a major character that it will be impossible to avoid some problems for passengers. The scope of the work has been described by the General Manager of the Southern Region as 'virtually rebuilding the M1 in railway terms', and it is intended to give the Brighton line travellers a rebuilt railway using 'one of the most technologically advanced control systems in the world'.

The benefit of these works will not be fully appreciated by passengers until the end of the 1980s and, meanwhile, delay and inconvenience will be unavoidable. In this brief book, I hope that I will be able to assist Central Division passengers to understand the present modernisation plans of the Southern Region, to appreciate the problems that will be faced in the short-term whilst modernisation work is carried out, and to enjoy their journeys by greater knowledge of the history of the line. I acknowledge with gratitude the help which I have received from Bob Mackmurdie and his staff in the preparation of the book.

C. S. Heaps LL.B.
Dorking, Surrey
March, 1982

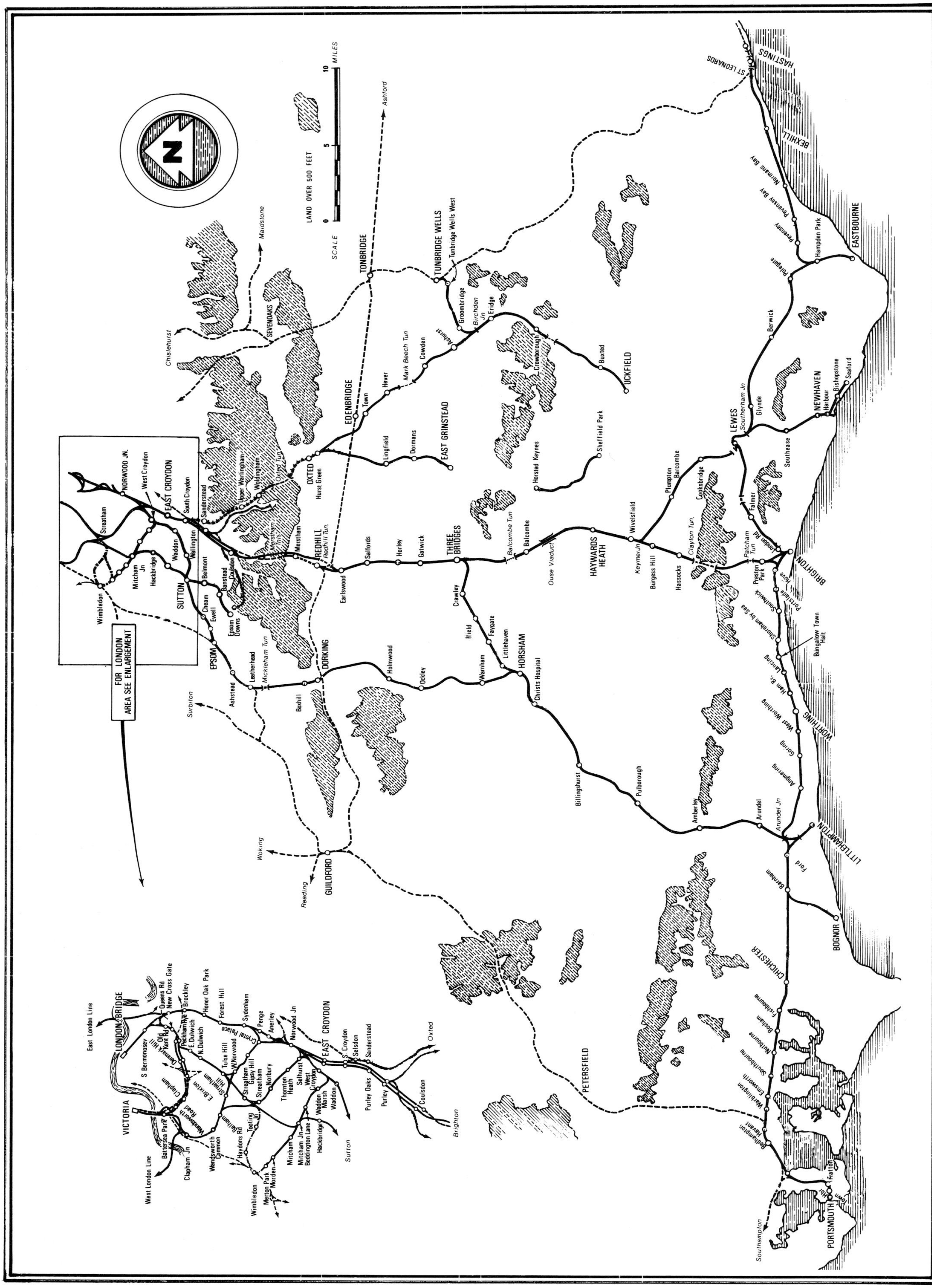
LAND OVER 500 FEET
SCALE
MILES
FOR LONDON AREA SEE ENLARGEMENT
LONDON BRIDGE
VICTORIA
East London Line
West London Line
Clapham Jn
Battersea Park
Wandsworth Road
Wandsworth Common
Clapham
S Bermondsey
Old Kent Rd
Queens Rd
New Cross Gate
Brockley
Peckham Rye
E.Dulwich
N.Dulwich
Honor Oak Park
Forest Hill
Sydenham
Penge
Anerley
Crystal Palace
Norwood Jn
Tulse Hill
E.Brixton
Streatham Hill
Balham
W.Norwood
Gipsy Hill
Streatham
Streatham Common
Norbury
Thornton Heath
Selhurst
West Croydon
EAST CROYDON
S. Croydon
Selsdon
Sanderstead
Purley Oaks
Purley
Coulsdon
Oxted
Brighton
Sutton
Tooting Jn
Haydons Rd
Wimbledon
Merton Park
Morden
Mitcham
Mitcham Jn
Beddington Lane
Waddon Marsh
Waddon
Hackbridge
NORWOOD JN.
West Croydon
Streatham
South Croydon
Sanderstead
Upper Warlingham
Woldingham
Oxted Tun
Wallington
Waddon
Mitcham Jn
Hackbridge
Belmont
SUTTON
Cheam
Ewell
Epsom Downs
Banstead
Coulsdon
Merstham
Merstham Tun
EPSOM
Ashtead
Leatherhead
Mickleham Tun
Surbiton
Boxhill
DORKING
REDHILL
Redhill Tun
Earlswood
Salfords
Horley
Gatwick
THREE BRIDGES
Crawley
Ifield
Faygate
Littlehaven
HORSHAM
Warnham
Ockley
Holmwood
Christs Hospital
Billingshurst
Pulborough
Amberley
Arundel
Arundel Jn
LITTLEHAMPTON
Ford
Barnham
BOGNOR
CHICHESTER
Fishbourne
Bosham
Nutbourne
Southbourne
Emsworth
Warblington
Havant
Bedhampton
Hilsea
Fratton
PORTSMOUTH
Southampton
PETERSFIELD
GUILDFORD
Woking
Reading
TONBRIDGE
Ashford
Maidstone
Chislehurst
SEVENOAKS
EDENBRIDGE
Town
Hever
Mark Beech Tun
Cowden
Ashurst
OXTED
Hurst Green
Lingfield
Dormans
EAST GRINSTEAD
TUNBRIDGE WELLS
Tunbridge Wells West
Groombridge
Birchden Jn
Eridge
Crowborough
Buxted
UCKFIELD
Sheffield Park
Horsted Keynes
Balcombe Tun
Balcombe
Ouse Viaduct
HAYWARDS HEATH
Wivelsfield
Keymer Jn
Burgess Hill
Hassocks
Clayton Tun.
Plumpton
Barcombe
Cooksbridge
LEWES
Southerham Jn
Glynde
Berwick
Polegate
Hampden Park
EASTBOURNE
Pevensey
Pevensey Bay
Normans Bay
BEXHILL
ST LEONARDS
HASTINGS
Southease
NEWHAVEN
Harbour
Bishopstone
Seaford
Falmer
London Rd
BRIGHTON
Patcham Tun
Preston Park
Hove
Portslade
Southwick
Shoreham by Sea
Bungalow Town Halt
Lancing
Ham Br.
WORTHING
West Worthing
Goring
Angmering

The London, Brighton & South Coast Railway

No doubt because of the density of its population and its proximity to London, the south-east of England in general, and probably the Central Division of the Southern Region in particular, has suffered less than most areas in Britain from branch line closures; although a comparison of the railway maps of Surrey and Sussex in (say) 1955 and 1975 will show that even this area has not totally escaped the Beeching axe. Minor branch lines apart, however, the boundaries of the Central Division vary but little from the railway system inherited in 1923 by the Southern Railway from the London, Brighton & South Coast Railway (LBSCR) which was itself made up of an amalgam of earlier lines including: the London & Croydon Railway; the London & Brighton Railway; the Croydon & Epsom, Brighton, Lewes & Hastings, and Brighton and Chichester companies.

The first section to be built was between London Bridge and (West) Croydon. The London and Croydon Railway Act received the Royal Assent in June 1835 — before Queen Victoria ascended the throne — which authorised the construction of a line between Croydon and a junction at Corbett's Lane (outside London Bridge) with the London and Greenwich Railway. The London and Greenwich was London's first main line railway which had been authorised by Parliament two years earlier and had already begun experimental running. The line of the Croydon Railway followed approximately the route and utilised much of the land of the Croydon Canal, which had opened as recently as 1809 but which had already become moribund. Its assets were purchased for the sum of £40,250, although the canal had cost over £125,000 to build! Using running powers permitted by its Act of Parliament upon payment of tolls over the London and Greenwich Railway to London Bridge, the London and Croydon Railway was officially opened on 1 June 1839 and made available to the public four days later.

Even before construction work had commenced between London and Croydon, envious eyes were being cast by others in the direction of Brighton, and between 1825 and 1835 numerous schemes were proposed for railways to the coast, including lines via Dorking, Horsham and the Adur Gap (near Shoreham); Croydon, Leatherhead, Dorking and the Adur Gap; Croydon, Oxted and Wivelsfield; and even between Croydon and Horsham through (or over) the North Downs at Betchworth. The 'direct route' through Merstham, Redhill, Horley and Three Bridges proposed by Sir John Rennie was finally chosen, despite an adverse report from Robert Stephenson who preferred an alternative line through Dorking proposed by Nicholas Cundy. Rennie's route was eventually authorised by the London and Brighton Act on 15 July 1837, but the Act received parliamentary approval only after the route had been approved by Captain Robert Alderson RE, an Ordnance Engineer requested by the Parliamentary Committee to study the four routes remaining under consideration and to make recommendations.

The fight for the route to Brighton had been intense and expensive, and the frustration and annoyance of prospective investors was clearly demonstrated by an extract from Herapath's *Railway Magazine* for April 1836 — a magazine for investors not enthusiasts — quoted in C. S. Dendy Marshall's *History of the Southern Railway*:

'Probably no subject has so much occupied the attention of the rail-road public of late as the rival lines to Brighton. Not less than six were some time since in the field at once — one by Sir John Rennie, a second by Mr Vignoles, a third by Mr Cundy, a fourth by Mr Gibbs, a fifth by Mr Stephenson, and a sixth by Mr Palmer, to which might be added the wild whims of some others that hardly arrived to a name before they died. At length the first two ceased to exist; Mr Cundy's, through sheer mismanagement, got hid under a cloud, and there only remained before the public the three last. Amongst these the fight was expected to be, when all at once Mr Palmer turned off from going to Brighton, to Dover, and left Messrs Stephenson and Gibbs to contend for the victory. Scarcely was this known to the public, before Mr Gibbs, owing to some irregularity or neglect, it is said, on the part of his subalterns, found himself so involved in dilemmas for non-compliance with the Standing Orders of Parliament, that his committee thought it needful to withdraw their intention of going for a Bill this session, and Sir John Rennie sprang up again to contest the point with Mr Stephenson. In this Bobbin-Joan sort of style it is that things have been going on with the Brighton lines, and such is the state in which they at present stand.'

A year later, Herapath returned to the fray. Mentioning that nearly £300,000 had already been spent in two parliamentary sessions, Herapath questioned whether it was right for Parliament to permit 'such immense sums of private individuals' money to be squandered' for merely obtaining parliamentary sanction which was 'as likely to be given to the worst as to the best line'.

The route eventually authorised commenced with a junction with the London and Croydon Railway near the Jolly Sailor (about half a mile south of Norwood Junction). The major earthworks required were a cutting over 100ft deep at Merstham, a 1,475ft long 100ft high viaduct over the River Ouse, and tunnels at Merstham (2,013yd), Balcombe (1,133yd), Haywards Heath, Clayton (2,266yd) and Patcham. The Ouse Valley viaduct designed by David Mocatta is now scheduled as a 'building' of historic interest, albeit one that is little appreciated by rail passengers. More obvious to observant travellers is the castellated northern entrance to Clayton Tunnel, which also incorporated a dwelling for a railway

Below: Smartly dressed invited crowds cheer the inaugural train as it leaves the Brighton Terminus on its journey to Shoreham on 11 May 1840. *Ian Allan Library*

Left: London, Brighton & South Coast Railway crest. *Ian Allan Library*

employee between its towers. This member of railway staff may initially have been employed to care for the gas lighting originally installed in this, and the other two longest tunnels, which were also whitewashed to assuage the fears of the travelling public then unaccustomed to being plunged into the bowels of the earth. This consideration for passengers was praised in the 1842 London and Brighton Railway guide in the following terms:

'Merstham tunnel is, as the other tunnels on this line are, whitewashed well throughout, and plentifully lighted with gas, which, though not of much value to the passenger (though, in him, it induces the feeling of confidence and cheerfulness), is, to the engine driver, of utmost moment, enabling him to see the road throughout almost as well as in broad day — so well, indeed, that any obstruction existing which otherwise could not be observed will by him be perceived and guarded against.'

With the combination of locomotive steam and gas jets, it seems unlikely that the whitewash remained effective for long!

The section of line between the Jolly Sailor and Haywards Heath opened to the public on 12 July 1841, but the section thence to Brighton was not ready until 21 September. Before that date, however, the inhabitants of Brighton had already begun to enjoy the delights of railway travel as the 1837 Act had authorised the construction of lines between Brighton, Lewes and Newhaven, and between Brighton and Shoreham. A single track branch (later doubled) to Shoreham had opened from Brighton 18 months earlier, on 12 May 1840. Shoreham and Newhaven had been included in the original proposals because they had established harbours; Brighton enjoyed no sheltered water suitable for shipping in all conditions until its Marina opened in the 1970s.

The Brighton line was one of the earliest main line railways to be built in the world, and it can claim an even older industrial lineage in that it incorporated, in part, the route of the Croydon, Merstham and Godstone Railway authorised as early as 1803 and opened (to toll paying horse-drawn vehicles) on 24 July 1805. Authority to purchase part of the route was contained in Section 40 of the London and Brighton Railway Act, and the older company was purchased in 1838 and finally dissolved in 1846.

The Brighton company procured access to London Bridge by exercising running powers over the lines of the London & Croydon Railway and the London & Greenwich Railway, to both of whom tolls were payable calculated by reference to the number of passengers travelling.

The immediate success for the London & Brighton Railway led to pressure for further railway building in Sussex. Although the statutory powers for the Newhaven branch were allowed to lapse, a new company — the Brighton, Lewes & Hastings Railway — was incorporated in 1844 to construct the coast line east from Brighton. With John Rastrick as its resident engineer, construction commenced quickly after the passage of the act and the line opened to Lewes in June 1846 and as far as St Leonards in November 1846. Branches to Newhaven and Eastbourne opened in December 1847 and May 1849 respectively. Travellers from Brighton on this line encountered the railway's major engineering work immediately after leaving the station, as the line swings eastwards over the 400yd long 27-arched curving London Road viaduct which stands 67ft above Preston Road and which to this day constitutes a major architectural feature of the town. The Lewes branch approached Brighton from the north, so prohibiting through-running from London, but this problem was resolved on the opening of a link from Keymer Junction (near Wivelsfield) to Lewes in 1847.

The eastern extensions were matched by developments to the west. Beyond Shoreham, the Brighton and Chichester Railway obtained powers in 1844 to construct a line to Chichester. As little major constructional work was required, other than bridges over the rivers Adur and Arun, the line opened as far as Chichester in June 1846, less than a year after the company had procured a further Act of Parliament authorising an extension thence to Portsmouth which opened in June 1847.

The main Brighton line, and the eastern and western extensions, formed the most important main lines of the London, Brighton and South Coast Railway (LBSCR), into which the Brighton and Croydon companies were amalgamated by a Consolidation Act in 1846. The new company purchased the shares of the Brighton, Lewes and Hastings and Brighton and Chichester companies (as well as the shares in the Croydon and Epsom lines), and thereby procured sovereignty over the major part of Sussex that now forms the Central Division of British Railways. The only remaining 'main lines' to be constructed were the 'mid-Sussex' branches through Horsham (then, and apparently still, considered secondary by railway management) and the very important section between East Croydon and Victoria. The London & Brighton Act 1845 authorised the construction of a line between Three Bridges and Horsham and this was opened in February 1848. The section thence to Hardham Junction (south of Pulborough) was built 11 years later as part of the Mid-Sussex Company's line to Petworth. This company was purchased by the LBSCR in 1862, and it was the LBSCR that determined to create an alternative main line to west Sussex by filling in the gaps between Ford and Pulborough (via Arundel) and between Horsham, Dorking and Leatherhead. The section to Arundel was opened in August 1863 and the line between Horsham and Leatherhead opened throughout in May 1867.

By the end of 1867, therefore, it can be said that the main structure of the present Central Division of the Southern Region had been constructed, as during the building of the mid-Sussex lines the LBSCR had also been completing the gaps in the line between East Croydon and Victoria over which the greater part of the Central Division traffic today passes. Increasing traffic into the joint London Bridge terminus of the LBSCR and the London & Greenwich Railway, including traffic from the South Eastern Railway (SER) both generally and over its main lines from Tonbridge and Reading via Redhill and East Croydon, had caused congestion even before the end of the 1840s, despite partial rebuilding and exchange of properties at London Bridge.

Meanwhile, London's 'West End' had become increasingly developed and popular with the travelling public, particularly following the success of the Great Exhibition in Hyde Park in 1851. Interestingly, Rastrick — the engineering chief of the London and Brighton railway — had forecast as long ago as 1842 that 'the Brighton will never be able to compete unless we have a line direct from our own line at Croydon to the west end of the metropolis'. The present apportionment of traffic between London Bridge and Victoria, particularly during off-peak hours, shows how correct his prophecy was to be.

The Great Exhibition of 1851 not only increased the attractiveness of the West End but also drew attention to the fact that the London Bridge terminus was inconveniently placed for access to that part of London — no underground railway had, of course, yet been opened. The rebuilding of the Crystal Palace at Sydenham in the following year by a company closely linked with the LBSCR by common directorships, inspired the directors of the LBSCR to concentrate on traffic potential in this area. Following the construction of an LBSCR branch from Sydenham into the Palace grounds in 1854, the independent West End of London and Crystal Palace Railway proposed an end-on link from Crystal Palace to Clapham Junction, with a view to an extension thence to the London and South Western Railway

Above: The final link in the line to London, between Haywards Heath and Brighton, did not open until 21 September 1841 by which time the main terminus building designed by David Mocatta had been completed. The fine building survives to this day, although its clean lines — evident in this early print — have been marred by a porte-cochère erected in 1882. This later addition, although no doubt unacceptable to architectural purists, provides welcome protection from the weather to passengers arriving at and departing from the station. The original train sheds protecting the platforms were designed by John Rastrick, the company's resident engineer. The original train sheds were replaced in 1882/3 when an elegant, curved iron-arched overall roof was erected on slender iron columns to provide a fitting gateway to England's most celebrated seaside resort. *BR*

Below: The terminus at Brighton was constructed on an awkward steep-sloping site. Both the commanding position of the new building and the local topographical problems are obvious in this print. At a later date, the forecourt was extended over Trafalgar Street and it was over this extension that the porte-cochère was partially built. *BR*

Above and below: The curving roof added to the Brighton terminus is conspicuous in this view of the station taken on 28 September 1977. In the middle Class 420 (4BIG) unit No 7032 stands at the head of the 14.45 non-stop service to Victoria (six months before an East Croydon stop was inserted in these workings) flanked by Class 423 (4VEP) unit No 7783 and Class 421 (4CIG) No 7322. To the left are the curving platforms serving the lines to the west — now designated 'Coastway West' on which Class 423 (4VEP) unit No 7781 was photographed on 20 July 1978 at the end of its journey from Portsmouth. Through workings from the west coast to the main London or east coast lines are rare, as the connections in platforms 2 and 3 are so situated as to enable only short trains to perform such a manoeuvre. *J. G. Glover; L. A. Nixon*

(LSWR) terminus at Waterloo, which was to be enlarged to accommodate both LBSCR and LSWR traffic. The LSWR wisely considered insufficient land to be available for such a joint terminus and in 1858 the Victoria Station & Pimlico Railway Company was incorporated to build a new terminus and a connecting line with the West End of London Railway at Battersea. This scheme was closely connected with the LBSCR and the new Victoria station (to be shared initially with the London, Chatham and Dover Railway and the Great Western Railway), opened on the site of the Grosvenor Canal basin on 1 October 1860. The line into the terminus crossed the River Thames on Grosvenor Bridge about 150yd downstream from Chelsea Bridge and was carried across the river by a four-span bridge supported on three piers giving a clear headroom of 22ft above high water. Because the Great Western Railway, then still wedded to its 7ft $0\frac{1}{2}$in broad gauge, planned to provide services into Victoria over the West London Railway through Kensington and Clapham Junction, mixed gauge tracks were initially provided.

The 'cut off' between Balham and Windmill Bridge Junction, near East Croydon, was authorised by the Croydon and Balham Hill Railway Act in 1860 and opened on 1 December 1862. It provided a

Top left: The connection to the east coast line from the London line causes no such problem, and the location of the junction some distance beyond the station is clear in this 1979 view of the approaches to Brighton terminus. In the middle, a 12-car train formed of 4VEP and 4CIG stock is departing for London, passing empty stock, electro-diesel (Class 73) and diesel (Class 33) locomotives and department stores unit No 023 in sidings on the site of the ex-LBSCR engine shed. On the right, partially blocking the view of the Preston Road viaduct, Brighton signalbox (which will be closed upon completion of the new power box at Three Bridges) stands precariously as the only remaining remnant of the ex-LBSCR locomotive works that formerly stood on the land behind.
Les Bertram

Above left: Like Mocatta's terminus building at Brighton, the 1839 Ouse Valley viaduct at Balcombe remains in heavy daily use almost 150 years later. Its elegant lines, and the Italianate pavilions decorating the approaches to the viaduct, are clearly visible in this 1977 view of a 12-coach Victoria-Brighton service formed of 4CIG/BIG units. *Les Bertram*

Below left: A northbound Brighton-Victoria fast service — identifiable by the headcode 4 — led by 4CIG (Class 421) unit No 7364 bursts into the daylight from the north portal of Clayton tunnel on 29 May 1977. The domestic dwelling incongruously perched above the north portal contrasts with the crenellated towers with which the tunnel mouth is adorned.
Les Bertram

Bottom left: The elegant lines and impressive size of the London Road viaduct at Brighton are very evident in this view of the 10.10am Tonbridge-Brighton service hauled by ex-SECR Class D1 4-4-0 No 31492, photographed approaching Brighton on 15 March 1958.
G. Daniels

shorter and faster route from the coast to the capital, but it was not until the end of 19th century that the final link in the present Brighton main line was forged, the 'Quarry Line' between Stoats Nest Junction (adjacent to the present Coulsdon North station) and Earlswood. For historical reasons, because the South Eastern Railway received parliamentary authority for its proposed line to Dover before the London and Brighton Railway Act was passed in July 1837, the Select Committee considering the later bill gave the SER the option to purchase the line actually to be constructed by the L&B between Coulsdon and Redhill (then an undeveloped area east of Reigate known as Red Hill) to avoid unnecessary duplication of lines. The SER exercised its rights to purchase on 19 July 1844, when a sum in

Top right: The 'direct' link from the Brighton line to Lewes, which opened in March 1847 and permitted through running without reversal at Brighton, left the main line three miles south of Haywards Heath. Despite being constructed in open country, the Lewes line at Keymer junction was built on a sharp 14-chain left-hand curve which to this day imposes a severe speed restriction on trains on the branch. The severe curvature is evident in this view of the 09.24 Ore-Victoria service photographed on 2 April 1978 headed by Class 421 No 7321 heading Class 410 buffet unit No 7005. In the background, on the main line, can be seen the platforms and station buildings of Burgess Hill. *Les Bertram*

Above right: The last section of the Mid-Sussex line to be constructed was that between Leatherhead and Horsham. The northern part of this section passes through the picturesque Mole Valley near Box Hill, and involved the construction of the short (530yd) tunnel under Norbury Park Mickleham visible in this photograph of Class 421 No 7314 at the head of the 11.02 Victoria-Bognor Regis/Portsmouth Harbour service photographed on 27 January 1978. Since May 1978, these services have been diverted via Crawley and Gatwick Airport, exposing passengers on the Dorking line to the rigours of surburban stock without lavatory facilities calling at all stations to London, and it is sincerely to be hoped that the quality of service referred to in the 'Commuters Charter' will be restored by the reintroduction of main line trains when the next Central Division timetable amendments are introduced in 1984. *John Vaughan*

Right: The close proximity of the LSWR and LBSCR lines at Clapham Junction, which no doubt led to the consideration of a joint terminus in the 1850s, can be seen in this view of the southern end of the station. On the left, four ex-LSWR lines lead to Wimbledon and the west; on the right the prototype refurbished Class 415 unit No 5401 leads a Class 416 two-car unit on the down-slow ex-LBSCR line on the 26 March 1981 15.49 service from Victoria to East Croydon. There is no physical connection between the two pre-Grouping railways at Clapham Junction. *Les Bertram*

Below: The Quarry line, opened in 1900, left the original LBSCR/SER joint line (via Redhill) at Stoats Nest junction, near the site of the present Coulsdon North station. In this 1968 view, two 2BIL units on an evening up service from Bognor Regis have just left Coulsdon South station (whose platforms can be seen in the far distance) and are approaching the junction with the Quarry line which can be seen to the right of the photograph. The through platforms at Coulsdon North which are just visible on the right are only used in emergencies, although its terminus platforms are presently served by peak hour suburban trains. Ministerial consent has been obtained for the closure of Coulsdon North, upon completion of the Brighton line resignalling scheme in 1984, and the line speed of the junctions on the Quarry line is being increased as part of this scheme from 50mph to 90mph. *J. V. Nickson*

excess of £300,000 was paid to the Brighton company as half the cost of construction work, and from that date onwards the L&B was in the unenviable position of having to run trains on its most important line over tracks owned by a competitor company.

Such an arrangement almost inevitably led to difficulties between the companies, especially when the SER found development of its services baulked by the amount of traffic generated from the Brighton line, and the Brighton company claimed that its trains were being delayed by SER inefficiency or perversity. The only long-term answer to the problem was to build a separate LBSCR line to avoid the main bottleneck at Redhill, and Parliamentary authority was obtained in 1894 for the construction of the new $6\frac{1}{2}$-mile line which, like the original line through Merstham, involved heavy and expensive engineering works. The new line ran parallel with the original railway, and the work again included cuttings up to 100ft deep, a 2,113yd tunnel at Merstham and a further shorter tunnel through sandstone at Redhill. Because of the development that had occurred between Redhill and Reigate since the coming of the railway 50 years earlier, the new line was taken to the east of Redhill, although as it commenced on the west side of the old line at Coulsdon as a continuation of the new extended local lines from South Croydon it had to cross the original formation in the cutting north of Merstham tunnels.

The avoiding line — or Quarry line as it is now known — opened to passenger traffic on 1 April 1900 and, in conjunction with quadrupling between Victoria and Croydon and south of Earlswood, provided by May 1910 four running lines all the way to Balcombe Tunnel, two-thirds of the way to Brighton. Plans to extend additional lines thence to Brighton, which would have involved the widening of the Ouse Valley viaduct and the construction of new tunnels through the South Downs, were reconsidered when suburban electric operation began and the Board was able to reconsider the need for such expenditure in the light of such experience and the prospect of electrification to the coast. The combination of the success of the suburban electrification experiment and the onset of World War 1 led to such grandiose plans being abandoned.

The mid-Sussex, and Balham-East Croydon, sections of the Brighton main line were not the last lines to be built by the LBSCR, but they can be said to have marked the completion of the basic system which still so well serves the modern traveller. In addition to the Quarry line, branch lines and secondary main lines continued to be planned and built in the second half of the 19th century by the LBSCR or associated companies — as between Three Bridges, East Grinstead and Tunbridge Wells and between Chichester and Midhurst — but the doubts about limited demand that delayed their original financing and construction have proved to be well founded, and many such branches have been closed and abandoned during the last 25 years.

There seems no prospect of a similar fate befalling the greater part of the remainder of the ex-LBSCR system that today makes up the Central Division of Southern Region and little further amputation seems likely.

The Atmospheric Experiments and Early Electrification

In 1982, 95% of the Central Division railway system is electrified, and travellers are accustomed to the intensive, regular and relatively clean services that have been provided on the main lines since before World War 2 and, in parts of the suburban areas, even before World War 1. Although, in the Inter-City 125 age, Southern Region passengers do not enjoy the standard of air-conditioned comfort now found elsewhere on British Railways, until fairly recently the Southern Region electrified system was considered one of the more modern parts of the nation's railway and, in the 1930s, it probably led the world.

The London & Croydon Railway was one of the first railways in the world to seek to find an alternative to the steam locomotive. Increasing congestion on its line and a desire to reduce working expenses led the directors to contemplate as early as 1840 the installation of the 'atmospheric system' developed in the late 1830s by Samuel Clegg and Jacob and Joseph Samuda. In short, the idea behind the atmospheric system was that trains should be propelled by atmospheric pressure as a vacuum was created in front of a piston in a tube laid between the rails. Each train was attached to its piston by an arm which passed through a slot in the top of the tube, and a vacuum was created by air in the tube being exhausted by pumps situated in lineside stations approximately three miles apart. With the noise and dirt of the steam locomotive restricted to such wayside pumping stations, a clean and silent form of transport was envisaged.

Experiments with the atmospheric system were carried out in 1840 on part of the West London Railway near Wormwood Scrubs, and the system was adopted by the Dublin and Kingstown Railway for its $1\frac{3}{4}$-mile extension to Dalkey upon which the atmospheric engines worked well after its opening in 1843. The Croydon company's engineer — William Cubitt — was not initially impressed by the atmospheric concept, but later agreed that the system might be suitable for the company's proposed extension from (West) Croydon to Epsom. Also, the construction of a new separate line from Croydon to London would enable a comparison to be made with normal steam working whilst alleviating the congestion on the line increasingly caused by a mix of suburban and main line services. The act authorising the construction of the Epsom branch included a clause enabling the atmospheric system to be used, and similar powers were granted to the Croydon company on whose lines the system was first to be installed, the new line to Epsom not yet having been constructed. Trial running commenced in August 1845 between Forest Hill and Croydon, but claims of high speeds and early success were soon followed by stories of mechanical failures that led to the deferment of atmospheric working for public use until January 1846.

In its early months the prospects for the atmospheric system seemed hopeful, and the combination of reasonable reliability and above-normal development in passenger traffic persuaded the board of the LBSCR, of which the London & Croydon Railway had become a part in 1846, to proceed with the introduction of atmospheric working between New Cross and Forest Hill early in 1847. The decision had not been made, however, without grave doubts being expressed about the reliability of the system, and even before the opening of the Stage II section the board had postponed atmospheric work on the proposed Epsom extension, which eventually opened in May 1847 using conventional steam locomotives.

The doubts and pessimism expressed by the LBSCR board speedily proved to be justified. Soon, weather conditions, both hot and cold, caused problems with the leather valves through which the piston arm passed resulting in loss of vacuum and, therefore, propulsion. The technology of the age could not match up to the demands of the atmospheric design, and on 4 May 1847 — within months of the opening of Stage II — atmospheric working was totally abandoned. This decision must have come as a nasty shock to the directors of the South Devon Railway, by whom a similar atmospheric system was to be introduced between Exeter and Teignmouth in September 1847. Indeed, this experiment proved no more successful and lasted for only about 12 months.

In 1847, therefore, the LBSCR reverted totally to the use of steam locomotives, and thoughts did not turn to alternative means of propulsion until increasing competition in the inner suburbs from the new electric tramways at the beginning of the 20th century led the Board to consider the question of electrification. Parliamentary powers were obtained in 1903 to electrify the system and the company's consulting engineer, Philip (later Sir Philip) Dawson, recommended the adoption of a German-designed single-phase alternating current overhead system suitable for both suburban and main line use. Contracts for electrification of the line from London Bridge to Victoria via Denmark Hill were let in 1906, and the first trial run took place on 17 January 1909. Public services began on 1 December 1909 using eight three-car (later converted to two-car) trains built by Metropolitan Amalgamated Carriage & Wagon Company

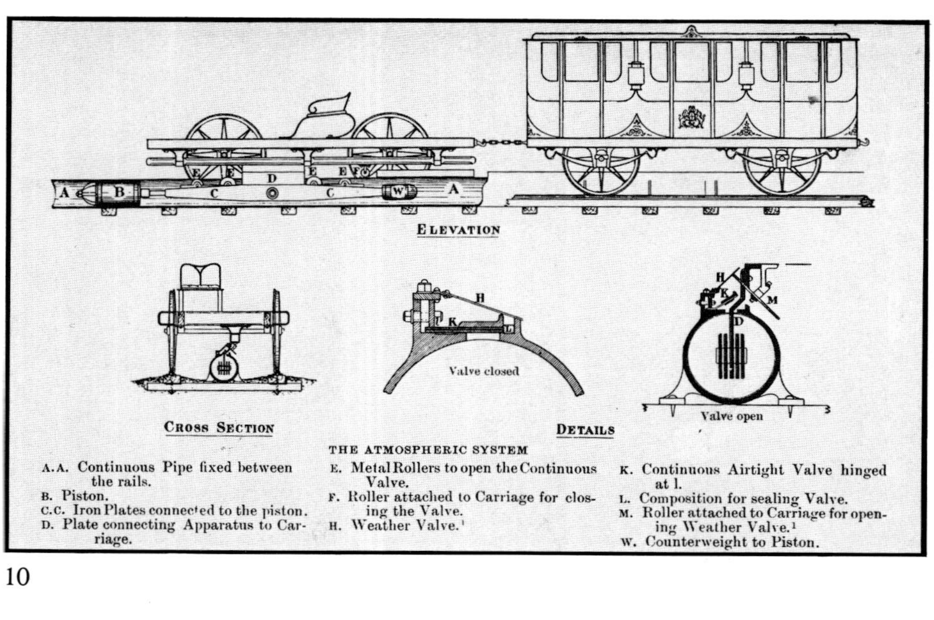

Left: A diagrammatic explanation of the atmospheric system. *Ian Allan Library*

Top right: Although the atmospheric system was abandoned by the LBSCR in 1847, some of the vacuum pipes remained in situ near West Croydon for 80 years until excavated by the Southern Railway in 1933. *BR*

Right: Even had the atmospheric system proved more reliable, it is doubtful whether the system would have been suitable for general railway use as the pipes and valves could not be adapted to operate in complicated pointwork. The need to avoid such problems led to the construction of the first railway flyover — flying junction — near Norwood Junction where the London Bridge-West Croydon-Epsom and London Bridge-Brighton lines diverged. *Ian Allan Library*

Limited of Birmingham. The speed of the new trains, 33% faster than the superseded steam services, so attracted passengers as almost to double, in one year, the traffic on the South London line to pre-tramway competition levels.

The manifest success of the electrified South London line naturally led the directors of the LBSCR to consider extensions, and electric trains were extended to Crystal Palace — via Streatham Hill in May 1911, and via Peckham Rye and Tulse Hill in March 1912 — using three-coach sets. Work also commenced on extensions to Coulsdon and Cheam, but this work had to cease because of problems in obtaining materials from German manufacturers on the outbreak of World War 1 in August 1914. After the return of peace, work was resumed on the Coulsdon and Sutton schemes in 1922 — notwithstanding the imminent demise of the LBSCR as an independent company on its incorporation in the Southern Railway on 1 January 1923.

On the formation of the Southern Railway, the new company inherited not only the overhead electric system of the LBSCR but also the 600V dc third-rail system introduced by the LSWR in 1915 between Waterloo and Wimbledon (via East Putney) and later on the Kingston 'roundabout', the Hounslow Loop and as far as Shepperton and Claygate. It would have been foolish to contemplate the long term use of different systems of electrification, and early in its existence the SR set up a committee to recommend the preferred system. In the event, the LSWR third-rail system was preferred to the LBSCR overhead system, mainly because of its lower installation and maintenance costs.

The ex-LBSCR extensions to Coulsdon and Sutton (recommenced in 1922) were, however, so far advanced that it would have been wasteful not to bring them into service, and work continued on these sections. They were opened on 1 April 1925, less than four months before another section of the ex-LBSCR, between Leatherhead and Dorking North, was energised on the third-rail basis as an extension of electrification from Waterloo. The running of through trains from Waterloo (ex-LSWR) to Dorking (ex-LBSCR) was one of the first manifestations of the benefits to be gained from the amalgamation of the previously independent railways that now formed the Southern Railway.

The extension of the overhead electrification to Coulsdon North and Sutton in 1925 necessitated the construction of new stock, and to these services 21 motorvans (nicknamed 'milk vans' to which the overhead collectors were attached) were provided to 'push and pull' 60 driving trailers and 20 trailers formed into five-car units (including motorvan). Following the decision to adopt the 600V dc system, these units were doomed to a short life and the total abolition of the overhead system was announced in 1926. Within two years, on 17 June 1928, the South London line had been converted to dc operation, and the last 'overhead' service train travelled from Victoria to Coulsdon North in the early hours of Sunday, 22 September 1929. This service marked the end of independent electric services on the Central Division, and from that date the suburban services on ex-LBSCR lines merely formed a part of the standardised 'Southern Electric' system that was rapidly being extended throughout the suburban area under the guiding hand of the Southern Railway's General Manager, Sir Herbert Walker. From 1929, so far as electric services at least were concerned, the LBSCR was visibly subsumed into the Southern Railway.

Below: An example of the stock used for the second phase of the 'overhead electrification' is seen in this view of a three-car Crystal Palace-Victoria service photographed passing Wandsworth Common on 17 March, 1928, 18 months before the total abolition of overhead electric working on the Southern Railway. The concrete bases upon which the supports for the overhead gantry were erected are still obvious to observant passengers alongside the line, particularly in the cutting south of East Croydon. *H. C. Casserley*

Above: This Victoria-Coulsdon North train, photographed approaching Windmill Bridge junction (north of East Croydon), is formed of two sets of 1925 'overhead' stock. The 'milk van' motor vans in the middle of each five-car set are easily distinguishable from the passenger stock. The lines leading to the right behind the leading driving coach lead to Norwood Junction and London Bridge. *Madgwick collection*

Below: Whereas new stock had been built for the 1925 'overhead' electrification extensions to Coulsdon and Sutton, stock that ironically was to be converted for use on steam-hauled services after only four years use, the coaches for the electric trains introduced for the replacement DC services were converted from ex-LBSCR, LSWR and SECR steam stock. Some of this converted stock remained in use until the end of the 1950s. The last units made up of ex-LBSCR converted stock, of which 4SUB No 4513 was a good example, were not withdrawn until January 1960. *Brian Haresnape*

Central Division Steam

Above: In its early years, like many other railways, the LBSCR purchased locomotive stock from outside contractors in small numbers and of differing designs. Locomotive superintendents came and went in quick succession until John Craven was appointed in 1847 to remain in charge for 22 years. He seemed to delight in numerous different types of locomotive, so much so that it has been said that a train spotter on the Brighton line in the 1860s could confidently have predicted that no Brighton train would be hauled by a locomotive exactly like its predecessor. It fell to William Stroudley to bring order out of confusion by standardising engines and components. One of his most famous designs, of which the prototype is preserved in the National Railway Museum at York, is the 'Gladstone' Class B1 0-4-2, an example of which, No 173 *Cottesloe*, was photographed taking water at Oxted on a Lingfield service. *Ian Allan Library*

Below left: Although the Class B1 'Gladstone' locomotives look frail, their ability to haul heavy express trains is evidenced by this photograph of No 197 *Jonas Levy* hauling the 'Sunny South Special' (formed of LNWR corridor stock) near Balham. The 'Sunny South Special', introduced in 1905, provided a through service in summer months between Liverpool, Brighton and Eastbourne and can possibly be regarded as a forerunner of the modern Brighton-Manchester service. *LPC/Ian Allan Library*

Below right: After Stroudley's sudden death in 1889 in Paris, where he was attending the Paris Exhibition, Robert John Billinton succeeded him and designed for the LBSCR the company's first passenger tender locomotives with leading bogies. To improve their performance, the B2s were rebuilt by Billinton's successor, D. E. Marsh, towards the end of the first decade of the 20th century. It is in a rebuilt form (as Class B2X) that No 213 *Bessemer* was photographed at Stoats Nest (Coulsdon) hauling a down Hastings Pullman express. *E. T. Vyse*

Above: D. E. Marsh, influenced no doubt by his training under Ivatt on the Great Northern Railway, favoured the Atlantic 4-4-2 wheel arrangements for both tender and tank locomotives. An example of his first class of express locomotives, No 40, is seen heading a down Brighton Pullman service which includes, immediately behind the locomotive, a six-wheel electricity generating van designed by William Stroudley to look like a miniature Pullman car and nicknamed a 'Pullman Pup'.

Left: The relatively short distances travelled by LSBCR expresses made them particularly suitable for haulage by tank locomotives of which Marsh's Class I3 4-4-2T must be considered amongst the most successful. Although modest in appearance, locomotives of this class were used on express services for many years and, despite the Southern Railway's electrification programme, many survived to be taken into British Railways' ownership. *Real Photos*

Bottom left: Marsh resigned through ill health at the end of 1911 and was succeeded by Lawson Billinton, son of Robert. His most successful design was Class K goods locomotive of 2-6-0 wheel arrangement. The modern appearance of Class K No 32343 photographed at Brighton in the early 1960s alongside 'Schools' 4-4-0 No 30917 *Ardingly*, belies the age of the locomotive built as long ago as 1916. *Brian Haresnape*

Top right: The last entirely new locomotive designed for the LBSCR was an express passenger tank locomotive, the Class L 4-6-4T. Seven of these powerful, fast and handsome locomotives were built, and the last — No 333 — was named *Remembrance*: 'In grateful remembrance of the 532 men of the LB&SC Rly who gave their lives for their country, 1914–1919'. One of the services upon which the Class L tanks were rostered with advantage was the 'Southern Belle' all-Pullman Brighton service, hauled here by Class L No 332. *Real Photos*

Right: Following the formation of the Southern Railway in 1923, a new standard express locomotive for use on main lines throughout the system was designed by the Chief Mechanical Engineer of the new company, R. E. L. Maunsell. The 'N15' or 'King Arthur' class was perhaps the most famous type of locomotive built by the Southern Railway, and a number were built with small six-wheel tenders specifically for use on the Central Division. When newly delivered, and before being fitted with smoke deflectors, 'King Arthur' class No 796 *Sir Dodinas le Savage* was photographed leaving Victoria passing beneath the overhead gantry and wires of the overhead suburban electrification system. *Real Photos*

Below: Many ex-LBSCR locomotives survived to be taken into British Railways' ownership in 1948. Many of the numerous 'E4' 0-6-2Ts survived into the last decade of steam (the 1960s), and No 473 *Birch Grove* has been preserved by the Bluebell Railway. The slightly younger 'E5' and 'E5X' classes were withdrawn in the 1950s. Class E5X No 32576 (originally named *Brenchley*) was photographed at Chichester in 1951. *C. R. L. Coles*

Main Line Electrification and the Pullmans

Just as the LBSCR led the way in southern England in introducing electric railway traction for suburban use, so it led the rest of the Southern Railway, and indeed the whole of the country, in developing main line electrification.

Following an announcement in the 1929 Budget by the Chancellor of the Exchequer (Winston Churchill) that railway passenger duty would be abolished if the capitalised value was spent by the 'Big Four' railway companies on improvements and other schemes intended to reduce unemployment, the Southern Railway announced in 1930 that its share of the duty (approximately £2 million) would be spent on extending electrification to the south coast. Including the cost of resignalling south of Coulsdon and station reconstruction at Haywards Heath and Brighton, expenditure of £2.7 million was anticipated, and work commenced on the electrification of over 150 miles of track in 1931. Electric services between Victoria and Three Bridges, and on the short section of the ex-SECR Reading branch extending from Redhill to Reigate, commenced on 17 July 1932, and the full service to Brighton was formally inaugurated on 30 December 1932 by a special train carrying local dignitaries and railway officials to Worthing and Brighton. Public services commenced on Sunday, 1 January 1933.

The stock introduced on these services will be familiar to passengers who travelled on the Central Division as late as the 1960s. For main line services to Brighton and Worthing, three basic types of multiple-unit trains were introduced. The most famous, and the longest lasting, were the three five-coach all-Pullman units (5BEL) built to replace the all-Pullman steam-hauled 'Southern Belle' introduced by the LBSCR in 1908 as 'the most luxurious train in the world'. Built by the Metropolitan-Cammell Carriage & Wagon Company, each five-coach unit was made up of two third class (later second class) motor coaches of 48 seats, two first class kitchen cars of 20 seats and one third class parlour car containing 56 seats. Each coach was painted in the traditional 'chocolate and cream' livery of the Pullman Car Company, to whom the supplemental fares payable on all Pullman services were payable. The Pullman cars were owned and run by the Pullman Car Company, but the vehicles were maintained by the Southern Railway.

Each first class car was adorned, in customary fashion, with a lady's name as follows:

Unit 2051 (later 3051) *Doris* and *Hazel*
Unit 2052 (later 3052) *Audrey* and *Vera*
Unit 2053 (later 3053) *Mona* and *Gwen*

The third class cars were merely numbered 'Car No —'. When originally introduced on 1 January 1933, the all-Pullman train retained the name of 'Southern Belle' — a name carried on roof-mounted boards on each coach — but 18 months later the name was changed (at the time of the introduction of the 'Bournemouth Belle' from Waterloo) to the 'Brighton Belle', the name under which it gained its popularity with the travelling public. The 'Brighton Belle' ran to and from London three times each day each weekday.

The other main line services to and from Brighton and Worthing were served by 23 six-car units made up of five ordinary coaches and one Pullman car (6PUL), and three similar six-car units which incorporated additional first class accommodation in lieu of Pullman facilities. Each of the Pullman cars was graced with a lady's name even though they were all 'composites' providing first and third class accommodation.

Below: An official photograph of two 5BEL sets forming the 'Brighton Belle' approaching Haywards Heath reveals clearly the Pullman Car Company coat of arms displayed on the cab ends, the roof-mounted name boards and the traditional umber and cream livery which adorned the train between 1933 and 1968/69. *BR*

Above: Another favourite spot for official photographs was on the Quarry line near Merstham. It was, however, a private photographer who captured 6PUL No 3002 in Southern Railway days on a Victoria-Eastbourne and Ore working. The bright sunshine picks out clearly the bright Pullman Car Company livery, and the detailed lining with which the units were originally adorned.
Q. J. Morris

The Pullman coaches used the following names:
Alice, Anne, Bertha, Brenda, Clara, Daisy, Elinor, Enid, Ethel, Grace, Gwladys, Ida, Iris, Joyce, Lorna, May, Naomi, Olive, Peggy, Rita, Rose, Ruth, Violet.

For stopping services, four-car units known as 4LAV were introduced, originally numbered 1921/53 but later renumbered 2921/53. Each motor coach contained seven third class non-corridor compartments, and the first class accommodation was contained in the intermediate coaches of which only one enjoyed corridor and lavatory accommodation.

Following the success of the Brighton/Worthing electrification, it was decided to electrify the lines to Seaford, Eastbourne, Hastings and Ore, and the branch from Haywards Heath to Horsted Keynes, at a cost of £1.75 million. The new electrified section was opened, with customary civic ceremonies, on 4 July 1935 and public services commenced on 7 July. The main line stock provided for the new services closely resembled that introduced in 1933, but in these new six-coach units a first class car with a pantry compartment (serving light refreshments) was substituted for the Pullman car. Although lacking the pleasing external colour scheme of the Pullmans, which contrasted brightly with the all-over green adopted for all Southern Railway electric units, these pantry cars in the 6PAN units were staffed by Pullman employees. To enable common facilities to be provided, coach rosters were altered to permit most 12-car trains to electrified coastal towns to be formed of a combination of 6PUL and 6PAN units.

For local services on the newly electrified lines, new two-car units were introduced designated 2BIL. Although both coaches in these units were provided with lavatory accommodation and side corridors, the coaches were not linked by corridors and (as indeed was the case on the main line stock) no access was provided between the units. Originally numbered 1981-1900, the first 10 units were later renumbered 2001/2010; the class eventually numbered over 150 units which saw service not only on the Central Division but also on the services from Waterloo to Alton and Reading and on the South Eastern Division.

The popularity of the new electric services was apparent not only to the travelling public but to the financial planners of the Southern Railway, who saw traffic on the Eastbourne/Hastings line increase by 22% within six months of completion. Inspired by yet further financial help provided to railway companies by the Government for developments in 1935, the SR next resolved to extend main line electrification to Portsmouth. The main line from Waterloo to Portsmouth (via Guildford) forms part of the South Western Division of Southern Region and is, therefore, outside the scope of this work, but the Mid-Sussex lines from Victoria via Horsham and Arundel to Bognor Regis and Portsmouth represent the last major section of the Central Divison to be so treated. In a way, the Mid-Sussex electrification was an extension of two earlier schemes. The line from Victoria to Epsom (via Sutton) had been electrified in 1929 to join up with a section thence to Dorking electrified as part of the Waterloo surburban system in 1925, whilst as far as Three Bridges on the Brighton line steam-hauled Mid-Sussex trains had passed over electrified tracks.

Public services were introduced on both routes on 3 July 1938, when electric services along the south coast west of Brighton were extended from West Worthing to Littlehampton. An hourly fast service via Sutton and Dorking was provided, dividing for Bognor Regis and Portsmouth at Barnham, where connections were also made with the Brighton-Portsmouth 'all-stations' coastal link.

For the Mid-Sussex lines, four-car units similar to those recently introduced on the Portsmouth main line were provided, although the restaurant car facilities enjoyed by passengers travelling via Guildford were replaced by Buffet cars staffed by Pullman Car Company employees. These new trains differed from earlier main line stock in that all coaches were provided with gangways not only within the units but at each end so that passengers could walk between all coaches and thereby enjoy the catering facilities provided elsewhere in the train. The design of the corridor connection at the driving ends of the motor coaches resulted in the destination headcode panel being placed to one side — balanced by the driver's window on the other side of the corridor connection — unlike on earlier units on which the headcode panel had been centrally positioned. These factors (no doubt combined with the destination of the units) soon earned them the nickname of 'Nelsons'. The units not provided with catering facilities were designated 4COR (Nos 3101-3158), and the buffet units introduced on the Mid-Sussex services were designated 4BUF (Nos 3073-3085).

The new services on the Mid-Sussex line had barely got into their stride before the Southern Railway was forced to face the problems of World War 2. On the Central Division, the most notable changes resulting from the outbreak of war were the almost immediate withdrawal of restaurant and Pullman facilities, the cessation of almost all non-stop Brighton trains and a general reduction in the frequency of services. In 1940, some Pullman facilities were restored,

but in May 1942 all Pullman coaches were withdrawn from SR electric services. The Pullman and other catering vehicles were withdrawn and stored, and Pullman cars were not restored to the Central Division until May 1946; a complete Pullman 'Brighton Belle' could not be provided until October 1947, when the unit (3052) damaged by a bomb at Victoria Station in October 1940 had been rebuilt and restored to its former glory.

After the end of World War 2, the pattern of services restored to the Central Division was very similar to that that had been provided in 1939, and even when the Southern Railway became part of British Railways on 1 January 1948 little changed. Despite livery changes elsewhere in the country, SR electric trains continued to be painted in their traditional green livery and, save for a substitution of the BR 'lion and wheel' crest for 'Southern Railway', a traveller in time transported from 1939 to (say) 1960 would have felt relatively at home on the Brighton line.

Top left: In British Railways' days, detailed lining was abandoned, and Southern Region electric units were painted in all-over unlined green, although during the 1960s the cab ends were partially or wholly painted yellow as a safety feature. 4LAV unit No 2949, photographed leaving Burgess Hill on 28 October 1969 at the head of a Victoria-Brighton stopping train, had been adorned with a small yellow panel and was destined to be withdrawn within 12 months. The 4LAV units were in daily use on Brighton line semi-fast and slow services for 35 years. *John Vaughan*

Left: Stopping services on the coast lines to the east and west of Brighton were generally formed of two-car units of which 2BIL No 2121, photographed on 21 August 1967 approaching Arundel, is a good example. From the pristine appearance of the all-over yellow cab front and roof, it would appear that this unit had been recently out shopped from works after an overhaul. No 2121 is attached to a 2HAL unit: — the 2HALs were made up of one corridor coach with lavatory accommodation and one non-corridor coach, and were used in common with 2BIL units on the Central Division in British Railways' days, although they had been originally designed for and introduced on the lines to Gillingham and Maidstone electrified in 1939. *John Vaughan*

Bottom left: The 'one-eyed Nelson' appearance of the 4COR stock built for the South Western Division electrification to Portsmouth and the Central Division Mid-Sussex scheme is conspicuous in this view of unit No 3114 leading an off-peak service from Portsmouth/Bognor Regis to Victoria approaching Dorking North during the 1950s, when main line Southern Region electric stock was still fitted with roof destination boards. The 4COR units were the first to be provided with corridor connections between units so as to enable passengers in all coaches to have access to restaurant facilities. *D. Sellmar*

Modern Rolling Stock

Above: The new suburban stock introduced by O. V. Bulleid for the Southern Railway at the end of World War 2 is still familiar to inner suburban passengers in the 1980s. Although the first units were designed to provide limited first class accommodation, such facilities were withdrawn 'temporarily' from inner suburban services on the outbreak of World War 2, and a policy decision to abolish first class on such services was taken before the great majority of 4SUB units were built. Unit No 4679 (now Class 405/2), photographed approaching Tulse Hill on 28 February 1975 on a London Bridge-Streatham-Crystal Palace-London Bridge service, was one of the later units to be built. The 'SHST' stencil beneath the driver's window indicates that the unit is allocated to Selhurst Depot. *Brian Morrison*

Below: The first inner suburban units to be designed and introduced by British Railways closely resembled the 4SUB units they were intended to supplement, although new braking and coupling systems prohibited their use in common with 4SUBs. The family relationship of the new 4EPB (Class 415/1) units with their predecessors can be clearly seen in this view of the fifth unit to be delivered, No 5005, approaching Norwood Junction at the head of the 11.41 Victoria-West Croydon service on 6 April 1978. In the background, Class 33/2 No 33.206, a narrow-bodied locomotive designed for use on the Hastings line, waits to leave Norwood Yard (closed in 1981). *Brian Morrison*

Save for Pullman passengers, who bewailed the loss of the personal attention and courtesy of the Pullman Car Company staff, most passengers on the Central Division were pleased to hear of proposals for stock modernisation when these were announced in the early 1960s.

Before then, only on the suburban services had modern stock been introduced. New steel-bodied four-car suburban sets designed by O. V. S. Bulleid were introduced by the Southern Railway in 1946 and continued to be constructed in large numbers by the Southern Railway and subsequently with minor changes by British Railways, designated 4SUB and 4EPB (now Classes 405 and 415 respectively) which will be familiar to all suburban travellers on the Central Division. The majority of the 4SUB units have now been withdrawn and the days of the surviving units are numbered, but the 4EPB suburban trains constructed by British Railways and built between 1951 and 1954 are now being given a new lease of life by the installation of strip lighting, new seating and improved heating to enable them to remain the mainstay of the inner suburban services until possibly the end of the century. Originally numbered in the 5001-5264 series, discerning passengers seeking greater comfort recognise these refurbished units by looking out for their new numbers in the 5401 (et seq) series.

Save for the 'new' four-car suburban stock, and similar two-car suburban stock (designated 2EPB and first introduced on the South London line in 1953 to replace the

Top left: It now seems likely that 4EPB stock will have to remain in service until the 1990s, and a programme of refurbishment commenced in 1981. Refurbished unit No 5403, resplendent in new two-tone livery, was photographed in deceptively sylvan surroundings near Wandsworth Common on 26 March 1981 on the 13.12 Epsom Downs-Victoria service.
Les Bertram

Above left: Most of the 4CEP (Class 411) main line units built by British Railways between 1958 and 1963 saw service on the South Eastern Division on workings to the Kent coast, but a number were allocated to the Central Division for use particularly on Mid-Sussex and rush-hour services until replaced by more modern stock. When photographed at South Croydon on 17 March 1979, unit No 7108 was unusually employed on the 11.23 London Bridge-Three Bridges (via Crystal Palace) service, a new service introduced in 1978 to improve communications with the Crystal Palace Sports Centre. Since the commencement of the 1981 timetable, these services have terminated at Redhill.
Les Bertram

Left: The 4CIG and 4BIG units delivered in 1964 were the first new main line units to be built for the Central Division since before World War 2. The BIG and CIG designations were chosen to retain a link with the LBSCR, as 'IG' was the old LBSCR code for Brighton, and the units were painted in customary Southern Region green livery. Newly delivered No 7313 was photographed at Victoria on 29 May 1965 preparing to depart for Eastbourne and Ore, and makes an interesting contrast with the 6PUL in the background. *S. Tallig*

Below: 4CIG (Class 421) and 4BIG (Class 420) units provide the mainstay of Central Division main line services today, and their appearance has been enhanced by the adoption of BR two-tone express passenger livery as worn by No 7432 leaving East Croydon on 17 March 1979 at the head of the 12.55 Victoria-Eastbourne service. Conspicuous in this photograph is one of the modern office blocks that have turned Croydon into a major commercial centre during the last 20 years, of such importance that in 1978 even the traditionally non-stop fast services to Brighton were retimed to include an East Croydon stop. *Les Bertram*

converted ex-overhead LBSCR trains) no new stock was constructed for Central Division workings during the early years of state ownership, or during the first phase of the British Railways Modernisation Plan announced in 1955. The majority of the new four-car main line units (4CEP and 4BEP) built between 1958 and 1963 were destined for the Kent Coast Electrification Schemes on the South Eastern Division. These saw electric services extended (under Phase 1) from Gillingham to Ramsgate, Sittingbourne to Sheerness-on-Sea and Faversham to Dover Marine, and later (in Phase 2) from Sevenoaks to Tonbridge, Dover, Folkestone and Ramsgate via Tonbridge, Maidstone and Ashford. Phase 1 opened to the public on 15 June 1960 and Phase 2 was completed on 18 June 1962.

The prototypes for the new main line electric stock were built in 1956 and ran for a short period on the Central Division, but generally the division was host to the new stock only on a temporary basis. This was particularly the case when numerous new units were stored on the division — as between Ardingly and Horsted Keynes where the branch was converted to single line operation to enable one running line to be used as a siding pending the vehicles' introduction on the Kent coast lines. It was not until 1964 that some early units of the 4CEP and 4BEP classes (these latter units including buffet facilities) were transferred to the Central Division to work services on the Victoria-Bognor Regis/Portsmouth line.

1964 marked a watershed on the Central Division. For the first time since before World War 2, brand new main line stock was introduced, to replace the fleet of six-car main line trains which had been introduced in 1933 and 1935 and each of which had travelled about three million miles. Fifty-four four-car units were constructed by British Railways at its York Carriage Works, 18 of which incorporated a buffet car to enable refreshment facilities to continue to be provided on the south coast lines, albeit without the ambience previously enjoyed by Pullman Car passengers. Subsequently, further similar units were constructed to replace the 1938 Mid-Sussex stock and these are the units used on all main line services on the Central Division today. With the exception of one single compartment, all second class accommodation in these units is provided in open centre-corridor saloons: 42 first class seats are provided in each set in compartments situated immediately behind the drivers' compartments. The units incorporating buffet car facilities (originally designated 4BIG and now known as Class 420/1)

Below: The 'Brighton Belle' retained its traditional Pullman Car Company umber and cream livery until 1968/9, but even before succumbing to the all embracing BR blue and grey livery (albeit with detail differences) the Pullman Car Company crest on the unit ends had been obliterated by yellow warning panels. When No 3053 was photographed at Brighton on 29 May 1968, the unit had been fitted with new two-tone air-horns (visible on the cab roof) and yellow warning panels: it was to be repainted in the new style within 12 months. *J. Scrace*

Top: By the end of the 1960s, almost all off-peak main line services on the Central Division were formed of modern stock, save for the 'Brighton Belle', whose 35-year old coaches continued to make thrice daily trips to and from Brighton. By 5 October 1971, when refurbished unit No 3052 was photographed heading for Brighton on the Quarry line south of Coulsdon — the original line via Redhill can be seen on the lower level at the right — the withdrawal of the Brighton Belle at the end of April 1972 had already been announced. *J. H. Cooper-Smith*

Above: In its traditional livery, each coach of the 'Brighton Belle' was easily distinguishable by its car number or name painted on the side of each coach, but after repainting 'Brighton Belle' was emblazoned on each coach and on the cab end. This new style is very evident in this view of No 3052 leaving Victoria at the head of the 11.00am service to Brighton on 29 June 1971, by which date all three units had been fitted with roller-blind route indicators in place of their original stencils. Since the completion of the Victoria resignalling scheme, the complicated trackwork evident in 1971 has been greatly simplified: all double and single slip points have been abandoned and only two scissor crossings remain. *J. H. Cooper-Smith*

can be distinguished by their numbering within the series 7031-7058: the non-buffet car units are numbered between 7301 and 7438.

As the new trains were delivered, the prewar train sets were withdrawn, and all Pullman cars (except the 'Brighton Belle') disappeared at the beginning of the summer timetable in June, 1967. Only the 'Brighton Belle' — reinvigorated by major refurbishment in 1968/1969 which sadly included the abandonment of Pullman livery and its replacement with a modified BR blue and grey colour scheme — carried on providing meals to passengers at every seat (including the service of kippers restored after a petition was organised for its retention in 1970 by Lord Olivier and other 'celebrities' to whom the 'Belle' was almost a second home). The kipper success was, however, short lived. In March 1971, it was announced that the 'Brighton Belle' would be replaced by normal stock in May 1972, and all the three units that had been the flagships of the line for almost 40 years saw final service on Sunday, 30 April 1972. Their last month in service was marked by excursions to unfamiliar territory, including visits to Seaford and over the Mid-Sussex line.

The abolition of normal Pullman facilities in June 1967 coincided with the introduction of the Bournemouth electrification scheme, for which four-car semi-fast corridor stock (4VEP) numbered in the 7701-7720 series was introduced. Externally, these units were superficially similar to the Brighton line main line stock, but each seating bay (unlike on the main line coaches was provided with an access door and the second class coaches were fitted with additional and therefore narrower) seats in a 3 + 2 formation. Following the delivery of the first 20 sets to the South Western Division for Bournemouth services, further units in the class (now Class 423) were built at York for the Central Division to replace the 4LAV coaches introduced in 1933, the last of which remained in service until 1969. The 4VEPs are numbered between 7701 and 7894, although 12 units have since been converted with increased baggage accommodation and reduced seating capacity for use on Victoria-Gatwick Airport services and renumbered

Above right: An official view of the refurbished interior of a first class coach on the 'Brighton Belle' in 1968. *BR*

Right: For semi-fast services, the 4LAV and 2BIL/HAL units were replaced by four car units designated 4VEP (Class 423). When originally introduced, the new units were delivered in all over blue livery as worn by No 7722 photographed near Balcombe on 31 May 1968 at the head of the 13.45 Victoria-Brighton semi-fast service. Subsequently, the 4VEPs have been painted in two-tone express livery, which is perhaps fortunate in view of the number of occasions on which they are to be found paired with main line stock. This ability to run almost all Brighton line stock in multiple gives far greater flexibility than was available before withdrawal of the prewar stock, on which the main line and semi-fast stock was not compatible. *J. Scrace*

between 7901 and 7912 (4VEG Class 427).

The only other 'main line' coaches to be found in use on the Central Division are two-car (2HAP, Class 414) units built in 1957/1958. Lacking corridor connections and first class and lavatory accommodation in 50% of the vehicles, these units closely resemble suburban units of similar vintage. Originally used on the Central Division mainly on south coast services between Brighton and Portsmouth, in recent years they have appeared more regularly — no doubt to the annoyance of regular travellers — on services between the south coast and London and provide a quality of ride substantially inferior to main line stock and little better (if better at all) than that provided by the 40-year old stock withdrawn in the 1960s. These units are numbered between 6001 and 6173, and even the adoption of main line blue and grey livery in which they are now being repainted cannot disguise their suburban origins.

In 1982, the 2HAP units on the Central Division were reformed into semi-permanently coupled four-car units, designated 4CAP (Class 413) numbered in the 3201 and 3301 series.

There is no immediate prospect of new main line stock being provided on the Central Division, although the 4BIG/CIG units are scheduled to enjoy 'refurbishment' to more modern standards of quality at about the time when they reach their 20th birthdays in 1985. These refurbished units are likely to resemble internally the refurbished Class 411 units (previously 4CEP) now in the use on South Eastern Division lines.

Above: Main line (4CIG) and semi-fast (4VEP) stock can also work in multiple with the two-car units (2HAP, Class 414) introduced in 1957/58, many of which are to be found on Central Division services on the lines along the coast to the east and west of Brighton. On one such service, the 9.32 Brighton-Portsmouth Harbour, Class 414 No 6062 was photographed passing Portfield Oil Terminal (near Chichester) on 13 May 1981. In the background, Class 33 No 33.034 awaits the road from the oil terminal siding. *Les Bertram*

Left: Central Division passengers will begin to enjoy standards of comfort and design more appropriate to the 'Inter-City' age when a programme of refurbishment of the 4BIG/CIG stock commences, upon completion of the modernisation of the earlier main line stock now in progress. This view of the interior of a modernised 4CEP (Class 411) second class saloon illustrates the new standards. *BR*

Specials on the Central Division

Above: Even in 1982, the Central Division of British Railways regularly acts as host to the Royal Family, particularly when providing special trains for the conveyance of visiting heads of state from Gatwick Airport to Victoria, and on Derby Day. The tradition that the Royal Family should travel to the races at Epsom by train is long established, as is shown by this view of Class I1 4-4-2T No 600 photographed at Epsom Downs station in 1907 at the head of the LBSCR five-coach Royal Train introduced by R. J. Billinton in 1897. *Ian Allan Library*

Above and below: Nowadays, the Royal Train provided for the Royal party on Derby Day may not be adorned with the Royal Coat of Arms and crowned lamps carried by No 600, but the pristine appearance of 'Schools' class 4-4-0 No 30926 *Repton* and its train photographed (above) passing Clapham Junction on 2 June 1961 heading for Tattenham Corner, and the appearance of Class 73 No E6036 photographed (below) at Victoria after hauling a special train for the Soviet Prime Minister Mr Kosygin to Gatwick Airport in 1967, clearly show that efforts are still made by the staff of Southern Region to prepare locomotives 'fit for a Queen' on such occasions. *J. Scrace; BR*

Above left: For a brief period, following the abolition of steam working on the Central Division, the Derby Day Royal Special was rostered to be hauled by one of the three Co-Co electric locomotives designed by O. V. Bulleid for the Southern Railway between 1941 and 1948. On 2 June 1965, the 'Royal' was hauled by a resplendent No 20002 and was formed of three Pullman cars and an ex-GWR 'Special Saloon' in chocolate and cream livery originally constructed in 1940 for VIP travellers' use and modernised in 1963 as an 'Executive Suite'. No 20002 carries headlamps as well as the (then) standard Victoria-Tattenham Corner headcode '38' to denote its Royal Train status.
J. Scrace

Left and below: Excursions to the Bluebell Railway may not have carried Royal or VIP passengers, but their locomotives were prepared to Royal standards. The ex-Caledonian Railway 'Single' No 123 photographed near Haywards Heath (left) may well have been the most unusual visitor ever to the Brighton Line when it was seen double-heading ex-LSWR Class T9 4-4-0 No 120 on 15 September 1963; whilst the ex-LSWR Adams 4-4-2T No 488 (built in 1882) photographed at Ardingly on the same day (below) was also a stranger to Brighton metals. In contrast, 0-6-2T No 473 *Birch Grove* was a member of R. J. Billinton's Class E4 introduced in 1897 which almost certainly had spent all its 60-plus years in service on LBSCR lines. Since the electrified passenger service between Haywards Heath and Horsted Keynes was withdrawn in 1963, the physical link between the Bluebell Railway and British Railways has been severed and through excursions to the Bluebell Railway are no longer possible.
A. G. Orchard; D. Cross

Below: The use of 'foreign' locomotives on the Southern Railway and the Southern Region was rare, although in British Railways' days some excursions to the south coast were hauled throughout by London Midland Region locomotives. On the ex-SECR Reading-Redhill branch, part of which falls within the Central Division, Western Region locomotives had limited but regular duties until the end of steam working at the beginning of 1965, as when 'Manor' 4-6-0 No 7808 *Cookham Manor* (now preserved) was photographed at Betchworth at the head of an excursion to the Central Division on 2 March 1963. *Dr D. P. Williams*

Above: Towards the end of steam operations on British Railways, locomotives from other regions penetrated the Central Division on excursions more regularly than in the years immediately following nationalisation. One such visitor, photographed taking water at East Croydon on 25 May 1963 at the head of an excursion from the London Midland Region, was ex-LMSR Class 5 4-6-0 No 44766. This was one of the very few members of the numerous 'Black Five' class to be fitted with a double chimney. The office building partially obscured by steam from No 44766 is Essex House, the headquarters of the Central Division of Southern Region. *Brian Haresnape*

Below: Even more unusual was the use of foreign dmus on excursion service on Southern Region, as on the occasion on Easter Sunday 1962 when three Metro-Cammell demus from the London Midland Region were photographed just north of Balcombe tunnel on an excursion heading for Brighton. *Brian Haresnape*

Brighton Line Modernisation

Just as a traveller in time transported from 1939 to 1960 would have seen little difference in the appearance of the rolling stock on the Central Division between those two dates, so he would have seen little contrast between the 1960 appearance of stations such as London Bridge and Victoria and their prewar state.

On the Central Division of Southern Region, stations still painted in green and cream paint continued in 1960 to serve green-liveried electric trains controlled by semaphore signals unchanged in appearance, and often in fact, during the previous 30 years. The same could not be said today. Following the initial replacement of Southern Railway green coach livery by an all-over blue livery adopted even for the main line inter-city Bournemouth stock in 1967, all Southern Region coaching stock (with the exception of the oldest suburban units) is now being repainted in the BR standard blue and grey livery which has been adopted for main line electric stock for over 10 years. On almost every station, Southern Railway signs and paint have been replaced by colour schemes and signs based on the BR corporate identity now so familiar to travellers.

New colour schemes and new signs are cosmetic in character and do little to improve the real lot of the travelling passenger. Far more important, and of course more expensive, are the major modernisation schemes that have been completed or commenced on the Central Division. The old, dingy and inconvenient joint station at London Bridge was rebuilt during the 1970s at a cost of £9 million, and was formally reopened by the Bishop of Southwark on 15 December 1978, 142 years and one day after the official opening of the first London Bridge station on 14 December 1836. In contrast to the depressingly poor facilities that were replaced, and as part of the £28 million resignalling scheme affecting not only the ex-LBSCR terminus at London Bridge but also the ex-SECR through-platforms serving Charing Cross and Cannon Street, the 'new' London Bridge incorporates a spacious new main concourse, the roof of which extends outside to cover the bus station, and a 30ft wide attractive covered footbridge linking all 16 platforms. The main train shed on the Brighton side serving platforms 9-16 has been retained and cleaned, and the architectural features of its ironwork picked out by an imaginative painting scheme.

The rebuilding of London Bridge caused some inconvenience to travellers, but it was possible to minimise much inconvenience to Brighton line passengers by closing the Brighton side of the station totally from time to time at weekends and by diverting traffic to other London termini. No such option is available to the Central Division in its plans for rebuilding Gatwick Airport and Victoria stations, two of the division's major projects for the 1980s.

Above: This 1975 view of London Bridge illustrates the rationalised track work resulting from the London Bridge resignalling scheme, and shows clearly the new covered footbridge linking the ex-LBSCR terminus and the ex-SECR through station, together with the office development that contributed towards the financial viability of the modernisation scheme. Since the photograph was taken and the new signalbox brought into use, further track changes have taken place following the demolition of the old signalbox seen on the right of the old photograph. *BR*

At Gatwick, the first phase of extensions to the station was formally opened by the Chairman of British Railways, Sir Peter Parker, on Thursday, 9 July 1981 and it is intended that the second stage of the rebuilding will be completed before the end of 1983 in anticipation of the introduction of a new self-contained Gatwick Airport-Victoria service in the spring of 1984. Gatwick

Above: The spacious and light appearance of the approach to the rebuilt London Bridge, and modern ticket office and travel centre facilities, are illustrated in this view of the terminus taken shortly before the formal reopening of the station by the Bishop of Southwark in December 1978. *BR*

Left: The close proximity of Gatwick Airport station and the original Air Terminal is well illustrated in this 1961 view of the (then) new Gatwick Airport station. 4LAV No 2940 is standing on an up working whilst 2HAL No 2684 pauses on a London Bridge-Brighton semi-fast service. *BUA*

Below: The working of the Victoria-Gatwick 'Rapid City Link' at Gatwick is dependent upon the reversible-line signalling arrangements introduced on the local lines in 196[illegible]. In this view taken on 13 April 1979, a Gatwick unit can just be seen at the far end of Platform 2, awaiting a rear portion from the south coast whilst meanwhile enabling airport passengers to join the train without haste. On the left, the Bognor Regis portion of the 11.05 service from Victoria formed of two Class 423 (4VEP) units — Nos 7730 and 7722 — departs from platform 1 leaving behind another 'Rapid City Link' unit to form the following service to Victoria. *Brian Morrison*

Airport is one of the major successes of the Central Division — the jewel in the crown — and the new station has been designed to deal with the seven million passengers per annum who it is anticipated will use the rail facilities when Terminal 1 at Gatwick reaches its full potential. At present, approximately 40% of all air travellers using Gatwick Airport travel to and from the airport by train, and it is hoped that this percentage will increase to 45% upon completion of the new rail facilities and the introduction of the proposed new train service.

Gatwick Airport station was built on the site of the old Gatwick Racecourse station, a little to the north of the original airport station (opened in 1935) which was closed when the new one opened on 9 June 1961. The new station adjoined the main terminal building, with which it was joined at first floor level by an overbridge and in which the railway ticket and information offices were situated. The new station was designed to deal with 12-car trains at three pairs of island platforms, and the work in 1961 involved the provision of a new up local loop line and the conversion of the existing up local lines into reversible lines to facilitate the attachment and detachment of separate Gatwick Airport (originally two-car) portions from the London end of Victoria-Bognor Regis services.

As mentioned in the railway press at the time, provision was made for later extensions 'if the volume of airport traffic should

Top right: The new travel centre and ticket office are illustrated in this view of the new concourse at Gatwick Airport opened by Sir Peter Parker in June 1981. *BR*

Above right: Even if the exhaust might suggest otherwise, the 2,580bhp of Class 47 No 47.445 provides ample power to haul the 09.25 Brighton-Gatwick Airport-Manchester Piccadilly service, photographed passing Horley on 8 July 1979. The two services in each direction each day are generally formed of six passenger coaches and two brakevans: the overnight service from Manchester and this morning service from Brighton do not enjoy refreshment facilities. *Les Bertram*

Right: The new Gatwick Airport concourse was only partially completed when a three-car cross-country dmu (Class 119) was photographed on 17 May 1980 leaving Gatwick Airport station. These services to and from Reading lay over in platform 6 at Gatwick Airport for almost 45 minutes between services, thereby enabling passengers from the airport to board without rush and to enjoy the comfort of a warm train in preference to a waiting room or windy platform. *Les Bertram*

warrant it', and this foresight has proved to be well justified. In 1982, throughout the day, four trains an hour from Victoria convey four-car portions for Gatwick Airport passengers and no less than eight trains an hour in each direction call at the station in off-peak periods, providing direct links from the airport not only to London but also to many towns on the south coast.

The extensions to the station for which provision was made in 1961 became clearly necessary as traffic volume increased in the early 1970s, and the new concourse opened by Sir Peter in 1981 forms a major part of the planned modernisation of the station. The new concourse is built upon a raft 'the size of a football pitch' above the platforms and incorporates a comprehensive travel centre and eight ticket issuing positions as well as staff facilities. Direct access to the raft can be obtained by staircases from all six platforms, four of which are also linked by reversible escalators to the raft.

Under Stage 2 of the rebuilding scheme, a second footbridge with escalators and stairs is being constructed on the north side of the original (1961) airport footbridge, and when this is completed and brought into use towards the end of 1982 it will then be possible to segregate arrival and departure passengers between the station and airport buildings. The cost of the new concourse and footbridges has been estimated to exceed £10 million, but the developing profitable traffic between the airport and the capital clearly justifies such expenditure.

Top left: The close proximity of Deepdene and Dorking (formerly Dorking North) stations is clearly shown in this view of Class 405 (4SUB) No 4641 entering Dorking (ex-LBSCR) station on a Horsham-Waterloo service as a cross-country dmu on a Redhill-Reading service passes over on its approach to Deepdene. *Les Bertram*

Above left: The 12 4-VEP units converted to provide additional luggage accommodation for Victoria-Gatwick Airport services and redesignated 4-VEG (Nos 7901-7912) can be identified by their distinctive livery. The livery incorporates the BR symbol and an aircraft logo and is conspicuous in this view of unit No 7908 photographed approaching Salfords on 10 May 1980. Second class passengers on these Gatwick Airport units continue to enjoy the luxury of curtains in each compartment, although curtains have been removed from 4VEP stock. *Les Bertram*

Left: In the Class 427 (4VEG) units, seats at the ends of the second class saloons have been replaced with luggage racks for airport passengers' luggage, and the luggage itself is shielded from the gaze of inquisitive passengers by blanked off windows. All the detailed variations unique to these airport units are visible in this photograph of a 4VEG captured off its normal track at Haywards Heath. *J. G. Glover*

In addition to the important, and growing, traffic between Gatwick and London, it was suggested in the 1970s that there was a demand for through services from Gatwick to other parts of the country, and this suggestion has already proved well founded. In May 1979, two through services in each

Top right: The competition — modern coaches, similar to this Green Line coach in its distinctive 'Jetlink 747' Gatwick-Heathrow Airport livery photographed at Gatwick Airport, and cheaper fares can attract custom away from British Rail's link from Gatwick to Victoria. Despite the longer journey time, the Green Line Southdown parallel coach service is particularly attractive to passengers travelling to and from the National Bus Company's Victoria coach station.

Right: The self-contained Victoria-Gatwick airport service to be introduced in 1984 will be powered by Class 73 electro-diesel locomotives converted for push-pull operation. Although it is hoped that more modern coaching stock will be used, such trains will resemble this 28 September 1979 view of No 73.139 photographed near Horley on the 16.55 London Bridge-Brighton service, at the end of a short period when normal Southern Region multiple-unit services had to be supplemented during rush hours by a limited number of loco-hauled trains. *B. Denton*

Below: Pending the opening of a planned fuel oil pipe to the airport, aircraft fuel for Gatwick provides an important part of the Central Division's freight traffic. Modern bogie tank wagons heading for the airport are seen here hauled by Class 33 No 33.040 at the entrance to Denmark Hill tunnel on 18 February 1975. *Brian Morrison*

direction were introduced between Brighton, Gatwick Airport and Manchester and in May 1980 an hourly fast service was provided between Gatwick Airport and Reading. The Manchester services, which have been economically planned to operate using only two sets of rolling stock, presently provide services to the north from Gatwick departing on weekdays at 09.48 and 15.31, and the southbound services are scheduled to arrive at Gatwick Airport at 05.21 and 12.20. The apparently uncivilised hour of arrival of the overnight train from the north, which departs from Manchester at 23.30, is particularly intended to cater for the numerous 'package holiday' travellers whose flights are often scheduled to leave early in the morning. The Manchester trains are made up of six loco-hauled coaches and two parcel vans hauled by Class 47 diesel locomotives, and are routed from the Central Division to Merseyside via East Croydon, the West London line through Kensington Olympia, Reading, Oxford, Banbury, Birmingham and Wolverhampton. Although primarily designed for Gatwick Airport passengers, the trains actually terminate at Brighton and are becoming increasingly popular with non-airport travellers, particularly the aged with luggage etc, who prefer to eschew the higher speeds available to the north-west on the electrified services from Euston for the benefit of avoiding cross-London interchange by Underground or taxi. Buffet car facilities are available on the 07.27 Manchester-Brighton and 15.00 Brighton-Manchester services.

The desire of passengers to avoid crossing London from one terminus to another has led to the almost instant success of the Gatwick Airport-Reading service (via Redhill and Guildford) introduced in 1980. This service is worked by three-car 'cross country' (Class 119) diesel multiple-units, each of which is being refurbished in turn by the installation of modern lighting, new upholstery and the provision of additional luggage areas — clearly marked on the outside of each coach — to cope with

Top left: The British Caledonian Central London Air Terminal at Victoria, constructed on legs above the carriage road between platforms 15 and 16 in 1962, has already been demolished as part of the current Victoria rebuilding plans. In providing check-in facilities for passengers and luggage in London for Gatwick passengers, it showed the way for the larger terminal now being constructed over platforms 8-19 which is due to open in 1984. *British Caledonian Airways*

Above left: A view of the Brighton line platforms at Victoria in late LBSCR days. *LPC/Ian Allan Library*

Left: The 'kinks' in the platforms designed to permit two trains to be accommodated at the same time on one platform are clearly visible in this view of the Brighton line platforms at Victoria in LBSCR days. The escaping steam from Class B2 No 207 accentuates the overhead electrical equipment. *Ian Allan Library*

Above and above right: Modernisation at Victoria is epitomised by these two views: (above) the new travel centre opened at Victoria in 1976 and (above right) the Solari indicator installed on the south-eastern side of Victoria station. This is identical to a sister unit installed on the Central Division concourse. *BR; J. G. Glover*

Below: When the new rail-air terminal at Victoria is opened in 1984, airport passengers and ordinary travellers will be segregated on different levels. Meanwhile, limited special facilities for passengers travelling to Gatwick Airport have been provided in a separate lounge and ticket office opened in 1980 adjacent to platform 13. It is to be hoped that passengers are not misled as to the rolling stock used on the Rapid City Link by the illustration of the HST on the wall! *BR*

airport passengers' needs. The majority of the Gatwick Airport services call only at Redhill (for reversal) and Guildford, although pressure is being exerted upon British Railways to insert additional stops at Dorking (Deepdene) and Wokingham if such additional calls can be inserted without extending the running time of one and a quarter hours between Gatwick and Reading. In the longer term, is is hoped that the speed and quality of the service may be improved, possibly when main line rolling stock can be 'cascaded' upon delivery of new inter-city coaches on the Bournemouth main line.

At present, such proposals are merely pipe dreams, but plans are already in hand to improve both the quality and speed of the service between Gatwick and Victoria presently marketed under the 'Rapid City Link' brand name. This provides a regular 15-minute interval service to Victoria with a journey time of 40 minutes or a little less. It is serviced by four-car semi-fast electric multiple-units converted to provide additional luggage accommodation (4VEG, Class 427) attached to/detached from ordinary passenger services from/to Brighton, Bognor Regis or Horsham.

This facility is adequate, but by no means perfect. Not only are Gatwick Airport passengers likely to be delayed by problems affecting the portion of the train to be attached/detached many miles away elsewhere on the Southern Region but also, particularly in the rush-hour period, the amount of luggage carried by airport passengers can cause annoyance to commuters unable to find a seat, or even to get on board, when they find their way blocked by baggage from Bangkok and suitcases for Zanzibar.

Segregation of these two different types of passengers would be advantageous to both and the Central Division hopes to introduce a self-contained service providing a non-stop link between Victoria and Gatwick Airport with a journey time of about half and hour in the spring of 1984. The present plan is to convert modern air-conditioned rolling stock (to provide air-conditioned comfort for the first time on the Southern Region on a regular basis) to 'push-pull operation' similar to the system used between Waterloo and Weymouth, and between Edinburgh and Glasgow. Each self-contained train will be powered (at the country end) by a Class 73 electric locomotive hauling eight passenger coaches and a luggage van converted to a driving trailer so as to enable the train to 'turn round' at each end of its journey without delay. It is possible that the special Rapid City Link services will be graced with a non-standard livery, to distinguish them from normal service trains and to enhance their publicity value, publicity that has become the more important in the face of increasing competition from National Bus Company airport coaches that have been introduced since the 1980 Transport Act received the Royal Assent.

The introduction of the self-contained Gatwick-Victoria service is linked with, and dependent upon, reconstruction works at Victoria itself. Little was done to improve or modernise Victoria station during the 1960s, whilst uncertainty about the construction of a Channel Tunnel and/or a British Railways link to Heathrow Airport made long-term planning impossible. A decision not to proceed with either project enabled certain modernisation work to be carried out at Victoria in the early 1970s, the most obvious signs of which to the travelling public were: the enlargement of the concourse behind platforms 9-15; the abolition of the 'kinks' in platforms 10, 13 and 15 originally installed to enable two eight-coach trains to use the same platform at the same time; the construction of a new ticket office and travel centre; and the installation of a Solari indicator board. These works form part of a £45 million plan to renovate Victoria station and to resignal and modernise the tracks leading into the station (and Holborn Viaduct). This is part of the 'Operation Victoria' scheme under which 267 miles of track is to be controlled from one new signalbox at Clapham Junction. The resignalling work began in 1976 and is now almost finished. Recently, however, new plans have been announced for further work at Victoria that is likely to inconvenience passengers between now and 1984.

Authority was given in the summer of 1981 for the development of a new rail-air terminal for Gatwick Airport passengers at Victoria. The new terminal is to consist of a 'raft' above platforms 8-19 at Victoria directly linked to Eccleston Bridge to provide access for cars, taxis and coaches which will enable airport passengers (and their luggage) to be segregated from traditional rail passengers who will continue to use the concourse

Below: Old and new layouts at Victoria. The two additional platforms now authorised are not shown. *BR*

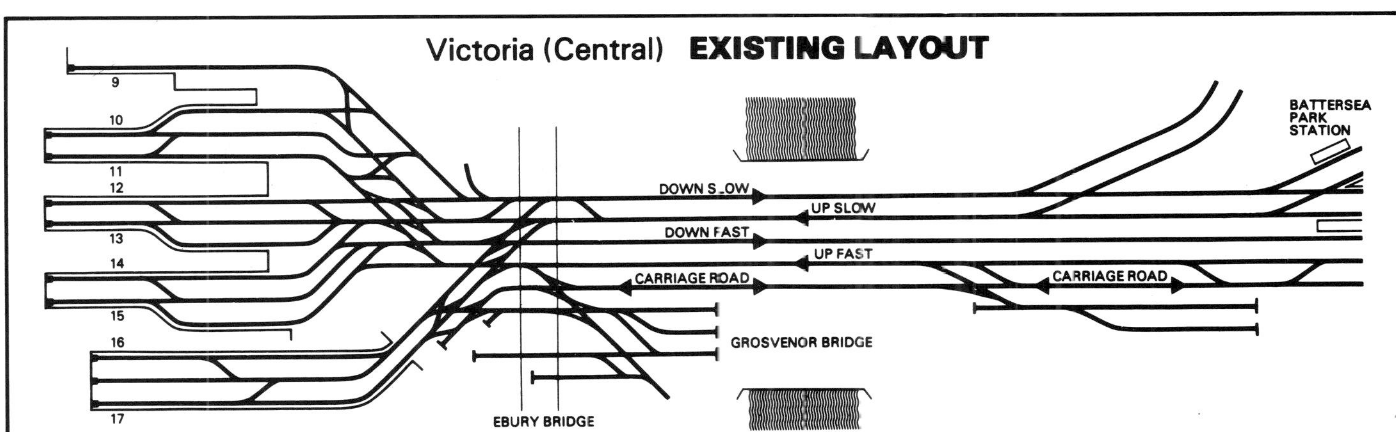

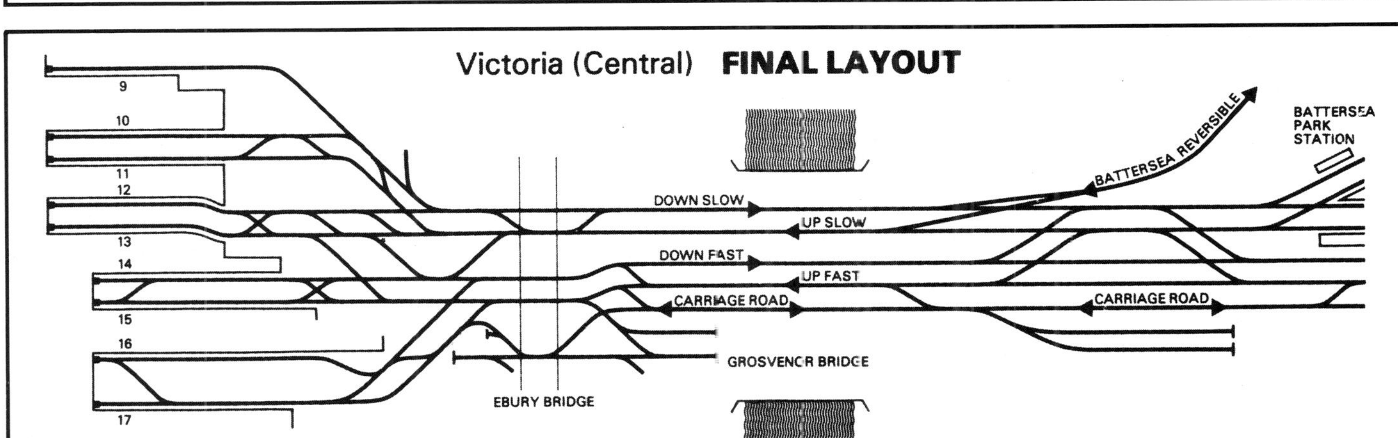

at platform level. The construction of the new raft will involve the demolition of the British Caledonian building (which was closed in November 1981 and then replaced by a temporary building on the concourse) and the new terminal will be provided with direct escalator and lift access to two new platforms (Nos 17 and 18) which will be used exclusively by Rapid City Link trains to and from the airport. The construction of the raft will involve boring 1,300 piles to a depth of 16m and, inevitably, will require certain platforms at Victoria to be closed for considerable periods of time and for additional platforms to be closed each weekend. It may tax the patience of Victoria passengers to put up with further rebuilding work at their terminus but in the long term it is is hoped that the new station will provide more convenient facilities for everybody.

Plans have also been announced for the development of an office building above Victoria station. Planning consent has been obtained for the construction of a five-storey air-conditioned office building with access from Buckingham Palace Road to be developed under an agreement signed in December 1981 between British Rail, Norwich Union Insurance Group and Greycoat London Estates Limited.

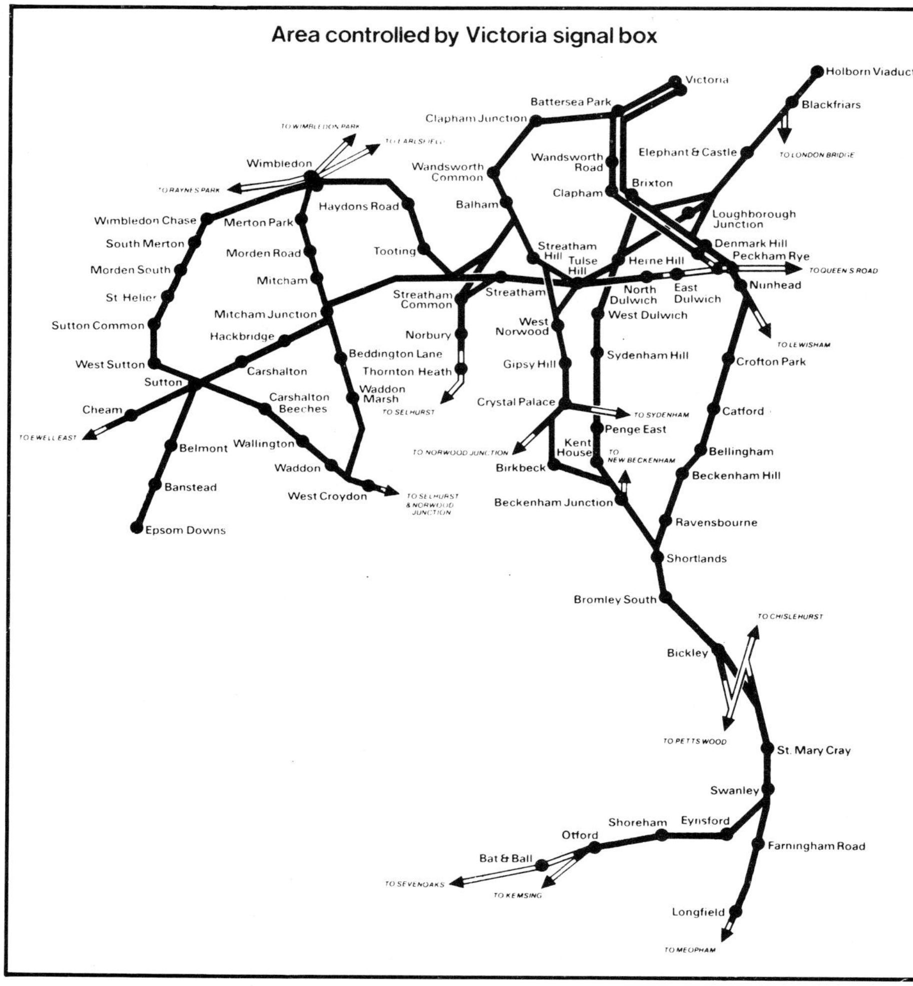

Right: Area controlled by Victoria signalbox. *ER*

Below: Artist's impression of the proposed Victoria station redevelopment. *BR*

Brighton Line Resignalling

Top: Signals installed by the LBSCR remained in use at busy East Croydon until after nationalisation. This impressive gantry of pre-Grouping lower quadrant signals at the north end of the station was photographed on 22 May 1951 before resignalling works had commenced. *P. J. Lynch*

Above: By 1955, colour-light signals operated from modern signalboxes at Gloucester Road junction and East Croydon had been installed, and this view shows the new signals erected on concrete cantilevered gantries about to replace the semaphore signals of which an upper quadrant example can be seen on the right of the photograph. The signalbox controlling the old semaphore signalling system was demolished upon the introduction of the new colour lights. *BR*

Right: The signalbox at Gloucester Road junction is a good example of the style of box erected between 1952 and 1954 when colour-light signalling was installed between Battersea and Coulsdon. The design bears a close family resemblance to the signalboxes built by the Southern Railway during the 1930s, of which examples can be seen at Horsham and Dorking North. *BR*

The Victoria resignalling scheme will come into full operation in 1983, when the new signalbox at Clapham Junction will control all Central Division services from Victoria as far as Beckenham Junction (via Crystal Palace), Thornton Heath (on the main Brighton line from Victoria) and West Croydon, Epsom Downs and Cheam (via Mitcham Junction). In addition the new box will control the single line branch from Wimbledon to West Croydon (via Mitcham Junction) and the loop line from Sutton to Tooting via Wimbledon. For the time being, the main Brighton line south of Thornton Heath through the complicated and busy junctions near Selhurst and through East Croydon will remain under the control of the relatively modern signalboxes constructed between 1952 and 1954 when colour-light signalling was introduced between Battersea Park and Coulsdon. South of Coulsdon North, the present signalling system was installed by the Southern Railway at the time of electrification to Brighton in 1933, when the new signalling comprised the greatest length of continuous track circuiting and complete power signalling on any British main line.

Much of the 1933 equipment is now almost life-expired and is incapable of renewal, whilst the age of the wiring makes it impracticable to bring it up to modern standards or to modify it to meet operating requirements.

As part of Southern Region's current signalling plan to control the whole Region from 13 signalboxes, authority has been given for the construction of a new signalbox at Three Bridges which will control: the whole of the Brighton main line from Thornton Heath (on the Victoria line) and Anerley (on the London Bridge line), together with the branches from Purley to Tattenham Corner and Caterham, and parts of the lines leading from South Croydon towards Oxted; from Three Bridges towards Horsham; from Wivelsfield towards Lewes; and eastwards from Brighton towards Lewes. Included in the scheme will be the section between Coulsdon South and Earlswood (via Redhill) which was excluded from the 1933 resignalling scheme and is still served by the traditional semaphore signals.

When completed, the new Three Bridges and Clapham Junction signalboxes will replace no less than 67 existing signalboxes, together with four further boxes which have previously been retained merely to operate level crossings. As the new signals are brought into operation, so the safety of passengers on the Brighton line will be further increased by the simultaneous introduction of British Railways' Automatic Warning System (AWS) which provides an audible warning to drivers of adverse signals.

Full resignalling of the whole line as far as Brighton will not be completed until October 1986, but it is hoped that all works north of East Croydon will be completed before the introduction of the new airport service planned for spring 1984. This section involves two major problem areas: the complicated junctions at Selhurst, where the Victoria/London Bridge and East Croydon/West Croydon lines meet; and East Croydon station itself. The whole railway network in this area is to be rebuilt, and the scale of the work has necessitated the introduction of a reduced Central Division train service from 5 October 1981. Already passengers will have noticed new track works and new signalling, as at Coulsdon where a new junction has been laid to increase the permitted speed on and off the Quarry line from 50mph to 90mph, but these works will pale into insignificance when compared with the major reconstruction that is shortly to commence.

In the triangle of lines between East Croydon, Selhurst and Norwood Junction, a new flyover for the slow Victoria line is to be constructed, together with two new bridges over the London Bridge lines to permit more efficient segregation of the two routes in the Gloucester Road area.

At East Croydon, the platforms are to be extended and widened so as to enable 12-car trains to be accommodated in every platform, and the track layout will be altered and sinplified to permit the four centre platforms to be used by trains in both directions. The extent of this rebuilding, which sadly will not include the reconstruction of the station buildings, is such that certain platforms will need to be closed for passenger traffic from time to time, whilst inevitably the major track and signalling work will necessitate speed restrictions on all lines throughout the rebuilding period. It is for this reason that a number of rush hour services were removed from the Central Division timetable or diverted to London Bridge in October 1981, as it was clear that the normal rush hour timetable could not be accommodated during the period up to 1984 whilst numerous speed restrictions and temporary longer signal sections reduce the capacity of the line.

This temporary inconvenience to passengers is regretted by British Railways

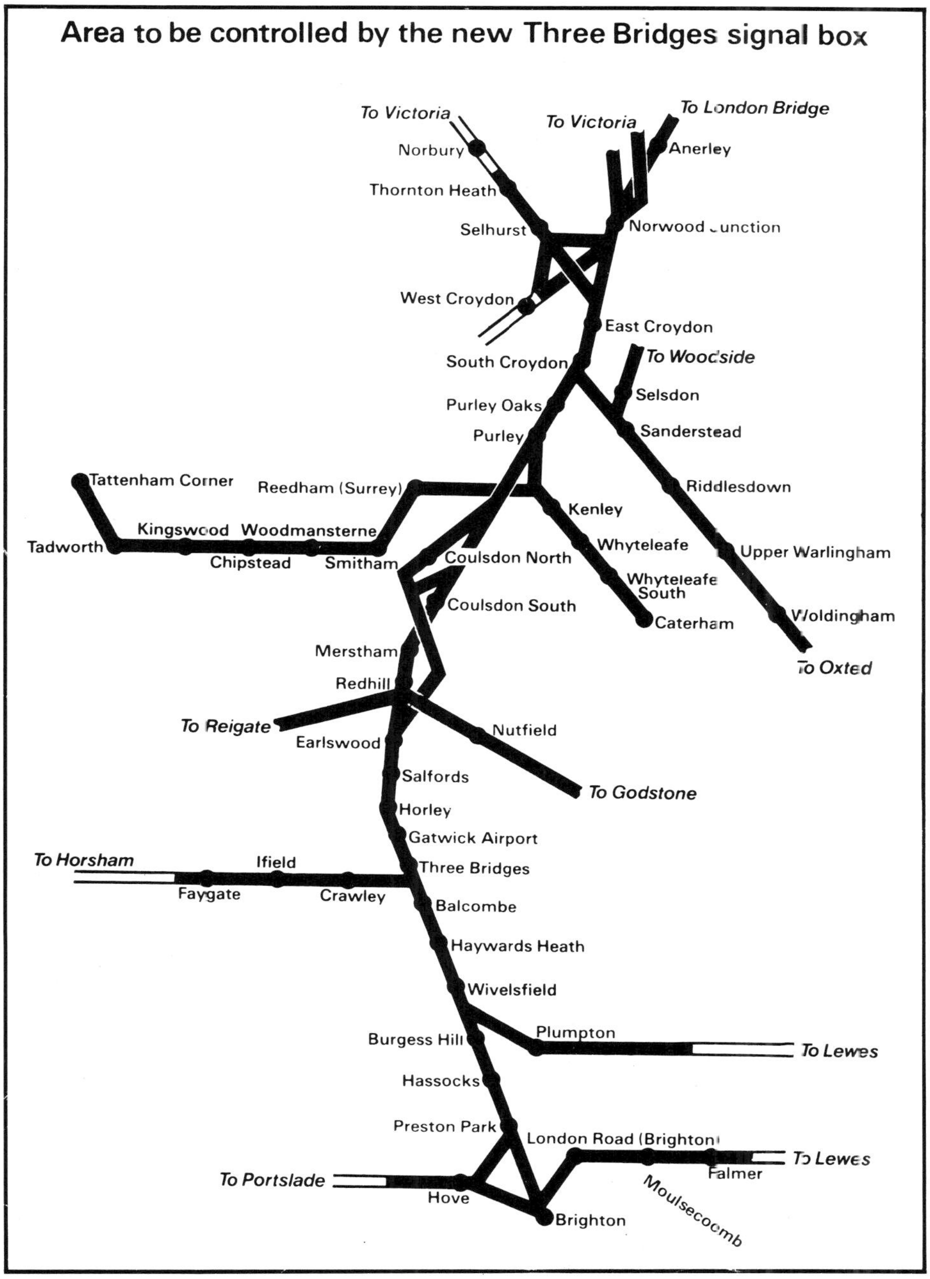

management but is unavoidable. Efforts are being made, however, to keep the travelling public aware both of the problems that are being faced and the progress of rebuilding by the issue of regular posters and bulletins under the heading 'Operation New Look'. Passengers will more readily endure delays and inconvenience occasioned by the rebuilding works if they are kept appraised of what is happening and can look forward to the more efficient and speedy service that is promised from 1984 when the works are completed.

Of particular interest to passengers in need of information about delayed or missing trains will be the introduction of visual display units (VDUs) in station staff offices which will be linked to the new signal-boxes at Clapham Junction and Three Bridges. These VDUs will enable station staff to identify the location and identity of individual trains at any point on the line, so as to enable announcements to be made about delays in running and platform alterations etc. Ultimately, 115 VDUs are planned, and already the area as far south as Coulsdon North is benefiting from this system based on information emanating from the Clapham box. Passengers at East Croydon, for example, may already have noticed the greater information that has been made available to passengers since VDUs were installed, when announcements have been made that a particular train is running (say) 15 minutes late or has just passed Balham.

Left: Area to be controlled by the new Three Bridges signalbox. *BR*

Below: Old and proposed new layout in the Gloucester Road Junction area. *BR*

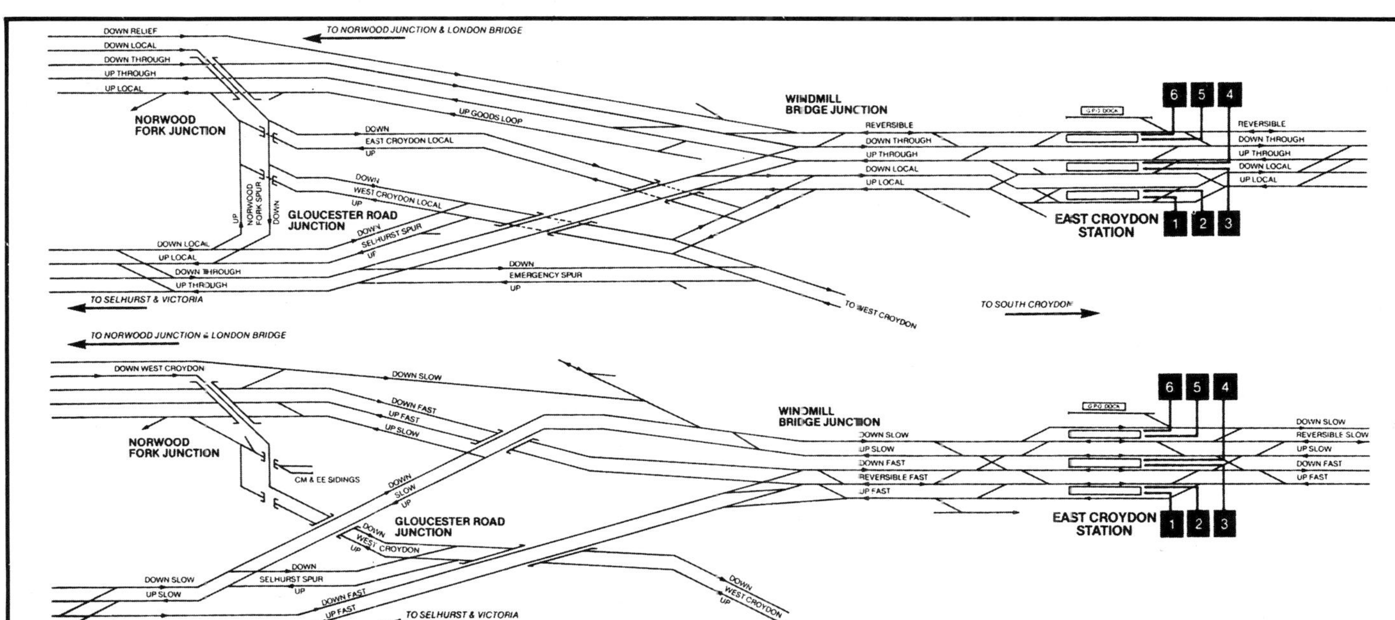

Above right: The new London Bridge signalbox, the first part of which was commissioned in July 1975, controls no less than 148 track-miles (47 route miles) where traffic is particularly dense during peak hours, and replaced no less than 16 old boxes. *BR*

Right: The rebuilding of the trackwork at East Croydon will remove the reverse curves that presently require a 30mph speed limit to be imposed on the 'fast lines' through platforms 1 and 2. The present S-bends and the sharp curve through the station platforms are visible in this view of 4SUB (Class 405/2) No 4689 leaving East Croydon at the head of the 16.10 Victoria-Coulsdon North service on 3 July 1980. The continuing growth of Croydon as an office centre is evidenced by the new building in the background (now completed and occupied) the construction of which had only just commenced when the photograph on page 22 was taken in March 1979. *Les Bertram*

Below: The complicated nature of the East Croydon/Selhurst/Norwood Junction triangle, and Selhurst carriage works, can be seen in the background behind Class 47 No 47.508 photographed on arrival at Norwood yard on 6 April 1978 with a coal train from Acton. Beyond, an up Tattenham Corner/Caterham-Charing Cross service has just passed under the flyover used by trains heading for West Croydon and Selhurst. The curve to Selhurst will be abandoned when the resignaling works are completed. The major works in this area will include the installation of a new flyover. *Brian Morrison*

Top: The terminus of the Sutton-Epsom Downs branch is one of the extremities of the area covered by the new Clapham Junction signalbox. By the time the box becomes fully operational, the branch will have been reduced to single track. The semaphore signals controlling Class 405 (4SUB) Nos 4678 and 4288 photographed leaving Epsom Downs on 25 March 1980 on the 16.12 service to Victoria ceased operation prematurely in November 1981, when the signalbox was destroyed by fire and an emergency shuttle service to Sutton had to be temporarily introduced. *Brian Morrison*

Above: A victim of the Brighton line modernisation scheme will be Coulsdon North station. At the public enquiry held by the Transport Users' Consultative Committee for London in February 1981 to consider the proposed closure of Coulsdon North station, many references were made by objectors to the good facilities and spaciousness of the terminus platforms at Coulsdon North which (it was said) compared very favourably with the facilities to be provided at the proposed alternative station on the Tattenham Corner branch, Smitham. The spacious platforms and generous awnings so appreciated by the objectors can be clearly seen in this view of 4SUB No 4283 arriving at platform 1 on the 8.46 service from Victoria on 4 November 1980. *J. G. Glover*

Left: The standard British Railways automatic warning system (AWS) is being installed on the Central Division as part of the Brighton line resignalling scheme. AWS gives audible warning to a driver of adverse signals, the warning being activated by magnets between the track that will be becoming increasingly familiar to regular travellers on the line. *BR*

Branches No More

Top: Many of the later-built, and picturesque, branch lines constructed by the LBSCR suffered under the 'Beeching Axe' and were closed to passenger traffic in the 1960s. A particularly famous branch line was that between Havant and Hayling Island (closed in November 1963) upon which the diminutive Stroudley 'Terrier' 0-6-0Ts (the first of which was built in 1872) remained in use until the end because of severe weight limitations over Langstone Harbour Bridge. When photographed during the last year of passenger services on the branch leaving Havant, Class A1X No 32662 gave no indication of its advanced years. No less than 10 locomotives of this class have now been preserved. *J. Goss*

Above: A picturesque branch whose closure may now be regretted is that between Christ's Hospital (near Horsham) and Guildford upon which LMSR-designed Class 2 2-6-2T No 41287 was photographed between Rudgwick and Baynards tunnel in May 1965. Development at Cranleigh — the most important station on the line — is now being inhibited by inadequate public transport facilities. *G. D. King*

Above: The branch between Polegate and Hailsham — the surviving rump of the 'Cuckoo line' between Eridge and Polegate — closed on 8 September 1968. On the last day of services, Class 205 'Hampshire' three-car unit No 1112 in its original green livery was photographed on the 11.16 Polegate-Hailsham working. *John Vaughan*

Below: One short branch line in Brighton itself which has had an interesting history was that serving the Kemp Town area to the east of the town to which a branch was constructed from the eastern end of the London Road viaduct in 1869. Although the branch was only one mile and 33 chains long, its construction involved the building of a 180yd long curved viaduct over Lewes Road and a 946yd long tunnel through the chalk ridge that runs parallel to the sea. The circuitous nature of the route meant that rail services could not compete with the development of bus services along the coast and passenger services were withdrawn as long ago as 2 January 1933. Goods services lingered on until June 1971, however, and the branch was a popular destination for rail enthusiast excursions. On 22 September 1967 Class 33 No D6529 was photographed leaving Kemp Town tunnel and entering the station yard hauling a non-powered four-car 4TC unit designed for use on a push-pull basis on the Waterloo-Bournemouth-Weymouth route. *John Vaughan*

The East Sussex Branches and the Oxted Line

Part of the LBSCR system which suffered most from the 'Beeching Axe' in the 1960s was the area to the east of the Brighton main line and south of Oxted. Resulting in part from competition in the second half of the 19th century between LBSCR and the SER, a complex system of secondary main lines and branch lines developed concentrated on East Grinstead and Groombridge (west of Tunbridge Wells). The first part of the network was a branch line from Three Bridges to East Grinstead which opened in 1855 (closed on 2 January 1967). The line was extended eastwards from East Grinstead to Tunbridge Wells and Uckfield in 1866. There then followed a pause in railway construction in this area until the 1880s. In 1880, a single line branch was constructed from Eridge to Hailsham and Polegate (to connect with Eastbourne): in 1882 the 'Bluebell Line' was opened between East Grinstead and its junction with the Uckfield line north of Lewes, and in the following year was linked to the main Brighton line by the short branch from Horsted Keynes to Copyhold Junction (near Haywards Heath). The final piece of the East Sussex Railway jigsaw puzzle was inserted in 1884, when the Croydon, Oxted and East Grinstead line opened to give the LBSCR, for the first time, an alternative route to Brighton avoiding the aggravation and congestion encountered on the section north of Redhill operated jointly with the SER.

In their heyday, these East Sussex lines (save for the Three Bridges-Groombridge section) were treated as secondary main lines and enjoyed through services between London and the south coast. They all survived beyond nationalisation but suffered under the Beeching Axe (and earlier) so that now the only sections to remain open to traffic are between: South Croydon, Oxted and East Grinstead; Oxted and Uckfield; and Eridge and Tunbridge Wells. Had the Southern Railway's plans for electrification not been terminated by the outbreak of World War 2, the position might well be different but the lines were never electrified and even those that remain open do not form part of the Southern Electric system.

Left: An early view of a LBSCR branch train on Oxted line duties, hauled by a tank locomotive whose appearance shows the pride with which locomotives were maintained in pre-grouping days.

As a result, these lines remained the last outpost of steam on the Central Division until dmus were introduced in 1962. These remain in service today. At regular intervals, the inhabitants of Oxted and East Grinstead are led to believe that an anouncement of electrification is imminent, but time and time again their hopes are dashed. It is to be hoped, however, that the opportunity for electrification will be grasped when the existing dmu trains require replacement.

Above left and left: During the days of the Southern Railway, many ex-LBSCR locomotives spent their declining years hauling trains on the East Sussex branches, and it was not until after Nationalisation that new and powerful tank engines were introduced on the more important services. Successful trials with ex-LMSR-designed tank locomotives led to their introduction on Oxted line services, where they were later joined by British Railways locomotives of similar design. (Left) Ex-LMSR Class 4 2-6-4T No 42099 was photographed on 21 May 1952 emerging from the short tunnel between Oxted and Hurst Green at the head of the 10.45 London Bridge–East Grinstead train. A 'close family relationship' is immediately apparent with BR Class 4 2-6-4T No 80153 (below left), photographed on 4 June 1960 near Oxted. *C. R. L. Coles; G. Kitchenside*

Below: Ex-SECR Class H 0-4-4T No 31518 seen at Three Bridges awaiting departure for East Grinstead on 2 March 1963. *M. J. Fox*

Above: Until the closure of the section of line between Uckfield and Lewes in May 1969, the pretence of main line status was preserved by the 18.10 Victoria-Brighton (via Oxted and Uckfield) service which was made up of main line stock and hauled by express locomotives. In June 1959 this evening commuters' express was photographed near Upper Warlingham hauled by 'West Country' class 4-6-2 No 34098 *Templecombe.* *J. Scrace*

Below: Many travellers on the Oxted lines, who still wait in hope for an announcement that their services are to be electrified, may not be aware that 20 years ago 'electric stock' was used for a short period on rush hour services. At the time when diesels of Class 33 were replacing steam locomotives on peak services and electrically heated coaches were at a premium, a seven-coach set of ex-electric coaches was formed, seen here approaching Anerley on 8 November 1963 forming the 07.25 Tunbridge Wells West-London Bridge (via East Grinstead) service hauled by Class 33 No D6528. The train was made up of two ex-2BIL driving coaches, and five trailer coaches from 4SUB units, in one of which first class accommodation was provided in a coach originally designed for composite use but which had been introduced to service as third class only following the abolition of first class facilities on inner suburban workings in September 1941. *Brian Stephenson*

Below: Nowadays, save for the occasional rush hour service made up of loco-hauled stock headed by Class 33 diesel locomotives, no pretence of main line status remains and all services are operated by three-car dmus. An example of this — Class 207 (3D) No 1311 — was photographed at Uckfield (now the terminus of the line) on 6 May 1980 preparing to leave for Victoria. From October 1981, all East Sussex diesel services have been diverted to London Bridge pending completion of the rebuilding of East Croydon and Gloucester Road junctions. *Brian Morrison*

The Bluebell Railway

It is perhaps ironic that the first successful standard gauge preservation society in Great Britain, formed to preserve and recreate the age of steam, should be found in Sussex, in the very midst of the Southern Electric system. The Bluebell Railway, which has now flourished for over 21 years and which sowed the seed from which so many other preservation societies have grown, runs regular steam services on the $4\frac{1}{2}$-mile section from Horsted Keynes to Sheffield Park which formed part of the ex-LBSCR branch from East Grinstead to Culver Junction (north of Lewes). This line opened on 1 August 1882 and was closed by British Railways, for the first time, on 28 May 1955. The last train should have run immediately prior to the commencement of the summer timetable in that year, but the closure was precipitated by an ASLEF strike that paralysed BR from 28 May, when it was generally believed that the line would not reopen.

A vigilant local resident, Miss Bessimer (related to the steel family) unearthed a clause in the line's original 1878 Act which had never been annulled and which required the LBSCR or its successor to run at least four trains each way a day, calling at specified stations. Miss Bessimer took the matter to law, and was successful. With ill grace, a passenger service was reintroduced by BR on 7 August 1956 — it did not reopen the most profitable station on the line as it was not mentioned in the 1878 Act — until it obtained Parliamentary consent for reclosure in 1958. But by this time the railway had attracted a lot of interest, and part of the line refused to die. Exactly a year after the second closure, a preservation society was formed at a well attended meeting at Haywards Heath and by the end of 1959 an agreement had been reached with British Railways to lease the line for seven years at an annual rent of £2,250. In May 1960, the railway's first locomotive — ex-LBSCR 'Terrier' 0-6-0T No 55 (BR No 32655) *Stepney* — was delivered: in July, the line was visited by an Inspector from the Ministry of Transport to satisfy himself that the line could be reopened without prejudicing the safety of the public. A Light Railway Order was granted on 15 June 1960 and the line officially reopened — for the third time of asking — on 7 August of that year. At the beginning, the Bluebell Railway was not authorised to run its trains into Horsted Keynes station, which then remained in the ownership of British Railways and was served by a two-car electric service from Haywards Heath, but from October 1961 it was permitted to run into the station to connect with the electric trains. After the electric service was itself withdrawn two years later, Horsted Keynes station became the sole preserve of the Bluebell Railway.

The Bluebell Railway has grown from strength to strength. In 1969 agreement was reached with British Railways for the purchase of the freehold reversion of the line for a price of £43,500. Thereafter, with this added security of tenure, its position as one of the leaders in the field of railway preservation has been secured and enhanced as each 'new' locomotive or piece of rolling stock has been delivered and subsequently restored to pristine appearance and working order. The locomotives now owned and operated by the Bluebell Railway range in age and size from the diminitive 'Terrier' No 72 *Fenchurch* constructed in 1872, to main line express locomotives constructed by the Southern Railway in 1945 and by British Railways as late as 1953. One of the line's latest acquisitions is a British Railways Class 9F heavy freight 2-10-0 locomotive, No 92240, which is presently being restored and which was not built by British Railways until 1958, after the Bluebell Railway had already closed for the second time!

Above: Following the second closure of the Bluebell Railway on 16 March 1958, the nucleus of railway enthusiasts who were to form the Bluebell Railway Preservation Society persuaded British Railways to offer to lease the line between Horsted Keynes (exclusive) and Sheffield Park for an annual rent of £2,250. One of the fund raising activities of the Preservation Society was the running of a 'Bluebell Special' which ran over the (now closed) northern section of the line. Hauled by ex-LBSCR ClassC2X 0-6-0 No 32535, the special train was photographed approaching East Grinstead on 12 July 1959, passing a well preserved ex-LBSCR signal. *J. C. Beckett*

The increasing number of locomotives and carriages on the Bluebell Railway is stretching to capacity the track and other facilities, and there are now hopes of extending the line northwards from Horsted Keynes to East Grinstead. The cost of reopening this section is likely to exceed £1 million, and the project is encountering some opposition from local landowners, but such a scheme amply demonstrates the optimism and enthusiasm with which the railway is looking forward to the future.

Details about membership of the Bluebell Railway Preservation Society can be obtained from the Membership Secretary, Sheffield Park Station, Nr Uckfield, Sussex.

Left: In the following year, on 17 May 1960, the Bluebell Railway took delivery of its first locomotive and carriages in confident expectation of the making of the British Transport Commission (Horsted Keynes and Sheffield Park) Light Railway Order 1960 obtained on 15 June. Ex-LBSCR Class A1X 0-6-0T No 55 (formerly BR No 32655) was photographed coming off the Brighton main line at Copyhold Junction en route to Sheffield Park. *E. Cross*

Below: It has been the policy of the Bluebell Railway to restore its stock and locomotives, so far as possible, to their original livery and condition and the high quality of such restoration is well illustrated in this view of 'Terrier' No 55 restored to LBSCR Stroudley 'improved locomotive green' livery. *C. Symes*

The first locomotives purchased by the Bluebell Railway Preservation Society were small and elderly tank engines, but subsequently the society has purchased, or been host to, larger locomotives of more modern design. All such locomotives have one thing in common, the quality of restoration which is manifest in these views of (left) ex-GWR 4-4-0 'Dukedog' No 9017; (below) ex-Southern Railway 'Schools' class 4-4-0 No 928 *Stowe*; (right) ex-Southern Railway 4-6-2 'West Country' class No 21C123 (BR No 34023) *Blackmoor Vale*; and (below right) British Railways' 4-6-0 Class 4 No 75027 seen near Freshfield Halt in September 1980.

A. E. Loosley; R. Sharman; Brian Morrison; P. H. Groom

21C123
SOUTHERN

75027

Central Division Headcodes

Below: Many of the headcodes in use on the Central Division were changed on the introduction of the 1978 timetable on 8 May. Before that date, headcode number 10, carried here by 4-VEP No 7799, indicated that the train, photographed at Earlswood crossing from the down Quarry line to the down slow line, was a Victoria-Gatwick Airport (via Quarry) service. Now headcode number 10 denotes a Victoria-Redhill/Reigate train. The telephoto lens accentuates the complicated track work at Earlswood, and picks out the semaphore signalling that still remains in use on the Earlswood-Redhill-Coulsdon South section. *Les Bertram*

Regular travellers on Southern Region will know that the route, character and destination of Southern Electric services can be determined by reference to the headcode carried by each train.

Destination headcodes were a feature of the 'overhead' electric trains introduced by the LBSCR when its second route was electrified; the trains carried numbered headcodes made up of metal plates with white figures on a black background suitable for illumination at night. When electric trains were introduced by the LSWR in 1915, lettered headcodes were introduced, and this system of using lettered headcodes was adopted by the Southern Railway when the third-rail electric system was extended in the suburban areas in the 1920s — older passengers might remember the advertisement for a well known bread manufacturer illustrated by five ex-LSWR electric units bearing the respective headcodes HOVIS.

New numbered headcodes were introduced when the 'overhead' electric system was extended to Sutton and Coulsdon North in 1925, and it was perhaps almost inevitable that numbers should be preferred to letters as the area of the Southern Electric system grew in the 1920s and 1930s and the advantage of having a choice of 99 numbers as opposed to 26 letters became apparent. When the Brighton line electrification was introduced in 1933, number headcodes were introduced, even numbers being used for trains to and from Victoria and odd numbers for trains to and from London Bridge. Although many individual route numbers were changed on the occasion of a major timetable reorganisation in 1978, the basic system introduced in 1933 still obtains on the Central Division as follows:

Where separate codes are not shown, trains terminating short of destination will carry the code for the throughout route. Quarry is the name given to the line avoiding Redhill.

Head-code	Trains between	Route
1	West Croydon-Wimbledon	Mitcham Junction
1	Redhill-Reigate	Shuttle
2	Victoria-Littlehampton	Quarry, Hove
3	London Bridge-Littlehampton	Quarry, Hove
4	Victoria-Brighton	Quarry-*Fast*
5	London Bridge-Brighton	Quarry-*Fast*
6	Victoria-Bognor Regis	Quarry, Horsham
7	London Bridge-Bognor Regis	Quarry, Horsham
8	Victoria-Portsmouth	Quarry, Horsham
9	London Bridge-Portsmouth	Quarry, Horsham
10	Victoria-Redhill/Reigate	
11	Brighton-Exeter	
11	London Bridge-Redhill/Reigate	
12	Victoria-Littlehampton	Redhill, Hove
13	London Bridge-Littlehampton	Redhill, Hove
14	Victoria-Brighton	Quarry-*Semi-fast*
15	London Bridge-Brighton	Quarry-*Semi-fast*
15	Waterloo-Horsham	
16	Brighton to Ore	
16	Victoria-Bognor Regis	Redhill, Horsham
16	Waterloo-Guildford	Bookham
17	London Bridge-Bognor Regis	Redhill, Horsham
17	Waterloo-Dorking	
18	Victoria-Portsmouth	Redhill, Horsham
18	Ore to Brighton	
19	London Bridge-Portsmouth	Redhill, Horsham
19	Waterloo-Epsom	
20	Ashford (Kent)-Eastbourne	
20	Victoria-Gatwick Airport	Quarry
21	London Bridge-Gatwick Airport	Quarry
22	Victoria-Littlehampton	Quarry, Horsham
23	London Bridge-Littlehampton	Quarry, Horsham
24	Victoria-Brighton	Quarry-*Stopping*
25	Holborn V/Blackfriars-Streatham Hill	Herne Hill
25	London Bridge-Brighton	Quarry-*Stopping*
26	Victoria-Bognor Regis	Quarry, Horsham, L'hampton
27	London Bridge-Bognor Regis	Quarry, Horsham, L'hampton
28	Victoria-Portsmouth	Mitcham Junction, Horsham
29	London Bridge-Portsmouth	Mitcham Junction, Horsham
30	Victoria-Gatwick Airport	Redhill
31	London Bridge-Gatwick Airport	Redhill
31	Tonbridge-Uckfield	
32	Victoria-Littlehampton	Redhill, Horsham
33	London Bridge-Littlehampton	Redhill, Horsham
34	Victoria-Brighton	Redhill-*Semi-fast*
35	London Bridge-Brighton	Redhill-*Semi-fast*
36	Victoria to Bognor Regis	Redhill, Horsham, L'hampton
37	Holborn Viaduct/Blackfriars-Sutton	Wimbledon
37	London Bridge-Bognor Regis	Redhill, Horsham, L'hampton
39	Holborn V/Blackfriars-W Croydon	Selhurst
40	Victoria-Norwood Junction	Selhurst
41	Redhill-Uckfield	Tonbridge
42	Brighton-Seaford	
42	Victoria-Littlehampton	Mitcham Junction, Horsham
43	Brighton-Eastbourne	
43	London Bridge-Littlehampton	Mitcham Junction, Horsham
43	Purley-Caterham	Shuttle
44	Victoria-Brighton	Redhill-*Stopping*
45	London Bridge-Brighton	Redhill-*Stopping*

Head-code	Trains between	Route
46	Victoria-Bognor Regis	Mitcham Junction, Horsham
47	London Bridge-Bognor Regis	Mitcham Junction, Horsham
47	Purley-Tattenham Corner	Shuttle
50	Victoria-Eastbourne	Quarry, Plumpton
51	London Bridge-Eastbourne	Quarry, Plumpton
52	Victoria-Newhaven Harbour Seaford	Quarry, Plumpton
53	London Bridge-Seaford	Quarry, Plumpton
55	Reading to Tonbridge	
56	Bognor Regis to Victoria	L'hampton, Horsham, Redhill
60	Brighton-Portsmouth	Direct-*Semi-fast*
60	Victoria-Eastbourne	Redhill, Plumpton
61	London Bridge-Eastbourne	Redhill, Plumpton
61	Littlehampton-Portsmouth	
62	Brighton-Portsmouth	Direct-*Stopping*
62	Victoria-Seaford	Redhill, Plumpton
63	Brighton-Portsmouth	Littlehampton
63	London Bridge, Seaford	Redhill, Plumpton
64	Brighton-Littlehampton	
65	London Bridge-Streatham Hill	Forest Hill, Crystal Palace
66	Brighton-Bognor Regis	Direct
66	Victoria-E. Grinstead	
67	Barnham-Bognor Regis	
68	Brighton-Bognor Regis	Littlehampton
69	London Bridge-West Croydon	Tulse Hill, Selhurst
70	Haywards Heath-Eastbourne	
70	Victoria-Selhurst	Crystal Palace
71	London Bridge-Coulsdon North	Forest Hill
72	Haywards Heath-Seaford	
72	Victoria-Coulsdon North	Selhurst-*Stopping*
72	Eastbourne-Ore *(carried by trains to and from Victoria)*	
73	London Bridge-Coulsdon North	Tulse Hill, Crystal Palace
74	Victoria-Coulsdon North	Selhurst-*Semi-fast*
75	Eastbourne-Ore *(carried by trains to and from London Bridge)*	
75	London Bridge-Coulsdon North	Tulse Hill, Selhurst
76	Bognor Regis-Littlehampton	
76	Victoria-Coulsdon North	Crystal Palace
77	London Bridge-East Grinstead	
78	Victoria-East Croydon	Selhurst
79	London Bridge-London Bridge	Tulse H, St Helier, Mitch Jn
81	London Bridge-Horsham	Forest Hill, Sutton
82	Victoria-Epsom/Effingham Junction	Mitcham Junction
83	London Bridge-Horsham	Mitcham Junction
84	Victoria-Horsham	Mitcham Junction
85	London Bridge-Epsom/Effingham Jn	Mitcham Junction, Forest Hill
86	Victoria-Beckenham Junction	Crystal Palace
87	London Bridge-Redhill	Tulse Hill, Crystal Palace
88	Tonbridge to Reading	
88	Victoria-Uckfield	
89	London Bridge-London Bridge	Mitch Jn, St Helier, Tulse H
89	West Croydon to London Bridge	St Helier, Tulse Hill
90	London Bridge-Victoria	Denmark Hill
91	London Bridge-Epsom Downs	Forest Hill
91	Wimbledon to London Bridge	St Helier, Forest Hill
92	Victoria-Epsom Downs	Selhurst
93	Charing Cross/London Bdg-Caterham	Forest Hill
94	Haywards Heath-Brighton	
94	Victoria-Epsom Downs	Crystal Palace
95	London Bridge-Brighton	Tulse Hill, Crystal P, Redhill
96	Victoria-Epsom Downs	Mitcham Junction
97	Charing X/London Bdg-Tat Cnr	Forest Hill
99	London Bridge-Uckfield	
08	Elmers End-Sanderstead	

Below: The latest suburban units (Class 508) delivered to the Southern Region for use on the South Western Division — which only see service on the Central Division on the section between Epsom and Horsham — do not sport the traditional Southern Railway headcodes but are fitted with destination blinds commonly used on other regions. Southern Region management has always imposed the strictest discipline to ensure the display of the correct headcodes, and many regular travellers hope that future new units will continue to display the traditional headcodes on which they have learned to rely, particularly as destination blinds — such as this 'Oxford' blind displayed by a refurbished Class 117 unit approaching Earlswood on a Reading-Gatwick Airport service — are treated (rightly) with less respect. Inaccurate blinds can be particularly dangerous at stations such as Redhill, where similar trains can leave from the same platform in the same direction for destinations as diverse as Reading, Gatwick and Tonbridge. *A. Dasi-Sutton*